CAMPOAMOR, SPAIN, AND THE WORLD

By

RONALD HILTON, M.A. (Oxon.)
Assistant Professor of Modern Languages
University of British Columbia

TORONTO
THE UNIVERSITY OF TORONTO PRESS
1940

THIS MONOGRAPH IS DEDICATED,
IN FRIENDSHIP AND RESPECT,
TO
PROFESSOR S. GRISWOLD MORLEY

CONTENTS

Chapter   *Page*

	Introduction	1
I	Traditionalist—Liberal—Reactionary	3
II	The Elusive Metaphysics of Campoamor	9
III	The Religion of Campoamor	26
IV	Philosophy of Art	43
V	Sociological Ideas	48
VI	Ideas concerning Government	54
VII	Philosophy of History	63
VIII	Race Theory	68
IX	The Primordial Races	72
X	The White Race—The Arab-Indian Branch	77
XI	The White Race—Caucasian Branch. Southern Group	80
XII	France	88
XIII	The White Race—Caucasian Branch. Northern Group. Germany	100
XIV	The Anglo-Saxons	108
XV	Spain	114
XVI	The Theorist in Practice	130
XVII	International Relations. Imperialism	134
XVIII	International Relations. Diplomacy	140
	Conclusion	143
	Index	145

COPYRIGHT, CANADA, 1940

SCHOLARLY REPRINT SERIES
Reprinted in paperback 2017
ISBN 978-0-8020-7066-1 (cloth)
ISBN 978-1-4875-9165-6 (paper)
LC 42-20005

INTRODUCTION

IN ORDER to survey the spiritual landscape of Spain, we first clambered hastily up the rugged hillside of Unamuno's works; we reached a lofty peak, on which the sun shone with burning brilliance, but the panorama below was blotted out by an acrid fog.[1] Proceeding somewhat up the valley of history, we reached the long and massive hump of Pardo-Bazan's *Obras completas*. Strolling more leisurely along its luxuriant crest, we were surprised by the sudden developments in the clear views which were afforded us.[2] At length we came down, counselling unprejudiced Hispanists to explore these abandoned forests where the paths have long been overgrown. From one point on the ridge,[3] we had caught a splendid vista of an eminence which is scarcely known save for a few pleasant foothills: Campoamor. We believed that its peak would offer a point of vantage from which to continue mapping out the contour of the landscape below. After an easy climb, for a tolerable path had been made the whole way,[4] we found that our hopes had not been in vain.

Like the fame of Pardo-Bazán, the reputation of Campoamor has suffered a rapid decline. The renown of the poet was flimsier and more ephemeral than that of Spain's most notable woman writer. It contained more enthusiasm and less respect. Most of his prose works and many of his dramas died young, whereas Doña Emilia's infinitely more copious production was uniformly living and vigorous. The integral value of Pardo-Bazán's work is beyond measure greater than that of Campoamor. Whereas the novelist deserves a splendid rehabilitation, the modicum of praise still accorded to the poet perhaps exceeds his merits. Apart from a few flashes of genius—to be found in his prose works—Campoamor is intelligently ordinary. This characteristic incidentally makes him most valuable for our study.

Campoamor offers a triple advantage as a lens through which to inspect the Spain of his day. (This comparison must seem odious to the shade of Campoamor, who used it mercilessly in his notorious quarrel with the Krausists, to whom he shouted *"A la lenteja!"*.) Although he is now considered as a poet, his prose work, buried in oblivion—this is the first study to give it real attention—completes our

---

[1]Ronald Hilton, "Unamuno, Spain, and the World." *Bulletin of Spanish Studies*, XIV (1937), Nos. 54 and 55.

[2]Ronald Hilton, *Pardo-Bazán, Spain, and the World*, (in press.)

[3]Emilia Pardo-Bazán, "Campoamor," *Retratos y apuntes literarios (Obras completas*, XXXII, 5-62). Most of the biographical details concerning the poet are taken from this study.

[4]The *Obras completas* of Campoamor have been published (Madrid: Felipe González Rojas, 1901-3) by U. González Serrano, V. Colorado and M. Ordóñez. This edition is always used in our references to the works of Campoamor.

picture of him as a man who incorporated, in an admittedly ephemeral way, all the spiritual and intellectual currents of his epoch: above all, the old religious traditionalism and the conflicting new scientific positivism. As his French contemporary Léo Quesnel said:

"Il lui fallait [à l'Espagne] un poète sorti du creuset des sciences positives. Biologiste, physiologiste, anatomiste et surtout chimiste par passion, Campoamor était, plus que tout autre, en état d'exprimer les préoccupations dominantes de l'esprit moderne; son cœur, naturellement tendre, était fait pour leur donner l'accent humain. . . . La gloire de Campoamor est celle d'un représentant, d'une incarnation poétique de la plus grande phase qui se soit encore produite dans l'évolution de l'humanité."[5]

That Campoamor represented the feelings and the thoughts of the Spain of his time is proved by the enthusiastic applause with which his fellow-countrymen greeted his works. Surveying this spectacle from the outside, Léo Quesnel could not suppress his amusement:

"Un étranger qui sans consulter l'œuvre poétique de Campoamor lirait ce qu'en disent les critiques espagnols, en viendrait à croire qu'il a paru derrière les Pyréneés un géant de la pensée. Rien n'égale l'enthousiasme, on peut dire l'engouement de ses concitoyens. . . . Grand poète, grand orateur, grand polémiste, profond philosophe, il est tout; il a le dernier mot de la science et de la sagesse humaines" (p. 213).

Finally, without being impeccably well-informed, Campoamor was deeply interested in the history and affairs of the world at large, and constantly strove to allot to Spain its correct place in his *Weltanschauung*. Although an unenlightened and cloistered xenophobia is definitely one Spanish viewpoint, it is not shared by the leading classes in Spain, however conservative. Certainly, a writer displaying this characteristic would offer poor material for a study of this kind.

---

[5]Léo Quesnel, "Littérature espagnole contemporaine. Ramón de Campoamor," *Revue Bleue*, August 14, 1886, pp. 213ff. Julio Cejador y Frauca, *Historia de la lengua y literatura castellana* (VII, 256), gives this date as 1882, and a number of critics have reproduced this error. It is also to be found in the *Enciclopedia Espasa-Calpe*, art. "Campoamor." The *Espasa* began appearing about 1908, although folowing a regrettable Hispanic custom intended apparently to prevent books' becoming antiquated, the date is not given. Volume VII of Cejador was published in 1917, so that the errors concerning Campoamor which Cejador and the *Espasa* have in common are probably due to the former's copying the latter, which is not a favorable testimony to Cejador's methods of compilation. Unfortunately, the articles in the *Espasa* are unsigned; there is a general list of contributors at the beginning of each volume. When in Madrid, I entered into fruitless negotiations with the Librería Espasa-Calpe to obtain information concerning the authorship of the individual articles.

CHAPTER I

TRADITIONALIST—LIBERAL—REACTIONARY

CAMPOAMOR's spiritual development followed a commonplace pattern. As a youth, he displayed a traditionalism tinged with the religiosity of adolescence. As a young man, he developed into a liberal of the intellectual brand, reading avidly and widely, and emitting a powerful flow of ideas. As he approached middle age, he degenerated into a conservative of the bourgeois type. He ceased to display originality in his ideas and became inconsistent and incoherent in the exposition of conservative divagations. This third phase was the most protracted of all, for Campoamor reached the age of four score years and four. However, our interest goes naturally to the second period; we are concerned principally with the structure of his ideas in these years of intellectual vitality. Yet we cannot neglect the dawn and the long twilight of his ideological development. We shall be constantly faced with the difficult problem of analyzing his *Weltanschauung* in itself and its development in time.

Ramón María de las Mercedes de Campoamor y Campo-Osorio was born in 1817, and grew up during the reactionary reign of Fernando VII. Even more than by his epoch, Campoamor's early life was conditioned by his home environment, which was such that the pious strain in him was inevitably stressed to the exclusion of other tendencies. Had he been born of noble or even bourgeois family, the liberal tradition which the 18th century had created in Spain would undoubtedly have reached him much earlier than it did. His mother was proud of her *hidalguía*, but Spanish feminine piety is common to all classes. Campoamor's father belonged to the peasant class and undoubtedly exuded the superstitiousness of Galicia and its borderlands. In any case, he died young, and little Ramón was left to the pious care of his mother and his aunt. The writer who was to become so exclusively *madrileño* was born in the Asturian village of Navia. Some five years ago, I found this lovely hamlet suffering from an attack of that political fever which spread epidemic-like through Spanish villages in the post-War period. Just over a century ago, however, it must have been isolated and sleepy, with little excitement save for ecclesiastical celebrations and the accompanying jangle of bells. Even bullfights had not yet become popular in the northwestern corner of Spain. Campoamor first studied

3

at Puerto de Vega[1] in an ecclesiastical college where religious ceremonial was strictly observed. Thence he proceeded to Catholic Santiago de Compostela. When, in his teens, he arrived in Madrid, where he was to attend the Colegio de Santo Tomás,[2] very few stains of unbelief must have blemished his immaculate piety. This is substantiated by his attempt to enter the Company of Jesus. He visited the Jesuit house at Torrejón de Ardoz, near Madrid, with this intention but abandoned his plans in dismay when he found that the Fathers, without inquiring after his humanistic achievements, examined merely his physical ability and his facility as a talker.[3]

The revulsion provoked by this episode marked the end of the early traditionalist period of Campoamor's life and the beginning of his liberal phase. Madrid, in those first years of the reign of María Cristina, was being swept by a wave of anti-clericalism which culminated in the *matanza de los frailes*, witnessed by Campoamor. For some two years, our budding writer studied medicine at the College of San Carlos,[4] which, like all centres of this discipline, was a home of unbelief. Abandoning the medical career, Campoamor, like most young Spaniards who needed an excuse for attending a university, turned to law and found himself in the midst of a group of young men indifferent perhaps to their speciality but generally interested in things intellectual. Having

[1]Puerto de Vega is a diminutive village situated on the Asturian coast between Luarca and Navia. It is known chiefly because Jovellanos, who had fled by boat from Gijón, threatened by the French, in November, 1811, put in there after a storm but quickly succumbed to a fatal attack of pneumonia.

[2]The Academia de Santo Tomás (such was its correct title), is described by Vicente de la Fuente, *La enseñanza tomística en España* (Madrid: Infante, 1874), 31-32. As the name implies, it was a Thomistic foundation, and it was doubtless as a reaction against his studies there that Campoamor developed his hostility toward theology and toward Santo Tomás in particular.

[3]The Jesuits should not be blamed too severely in the light of the persecutions they had suffered and were still suffering in 1834. After its recall by Ferdinand VII in 1815, the Society had been attacked during the Revolution of 1820. Twenty-five Jesuits had been slain at Madrid in 1822. Their status was restored in 1823, but in 1834 they were again the object of attacks in the capital. Fourteen were killed and the whole order was banished by the Liberal government on July 4, 1835. It was obvious, therefore, that they needed men of action rather than scholars. *Vide* J. H. Pollen, "Society of Jesus," *Catholic Encyclopedia.*

[4]The Real Colegio de Cirugía y Medicina de San Carlos had been founded in 1799, but its building had just been completed when Campoamor attended it. The Universidad Central was not definitely transferred from Alcalá to Madrid until 1836, and the Colegio de San Carlos was not made a Faculty of it until 1845. *Vide* Vicente de la Fuente, *Historia de las universidades, colegios y demás establecimientos de enseñanza en España* (Madrid: Fuentenebro, 1889), IV, 380.

decided that his future lay in literature, Campoamor devoted himself to reading assiduously and spent some five hours daily in the Biblioteca Nacional.[5] He does not seem to have kept up his reading habit, but this period of wide and intensive study left a clear mark in all his subsequent writings.

The first work in which Campoamor's liberal ideology manifested itself was his *Historia crítica de las cortes reformadoras* (1845).[6] It reveals a curious mixture of his early traditionalist nationalism and a radical liberalism containing an almost socialistic suggestion of a capital levy. The two currents are visible in the following whirlpool of metaphors:

"Es ocasión de lanzar un rayo de luz en el seno del caos adminis-trativo y, trazando límites a esa imagen de la eternidad, hacer una racional distribución de poderes para que todas las clases bien acaudilladas contribuyan a la erección de esa altísima columna sobre la cual hemos de colocar el sol de España, sobreponiéndole a la montaña de oro que debemos y que nos roba la luz que el cielo envía para fertilizar nuestros campos" (II, 33).

This work is decidedly immature. After subtracting the numerous *ad hominem* diatribes, the reader finds it difficult to say what Campoamor really thinks.[7]

Much more cogency and clarity are displayed in the short work which Campoamor published the following year (1846), entitled *Filosofía de las leyes*.[8] This work represents clearly the spirit and ideas of the *philosophes*, in particular of Montesquieu, whose *Esprit des lois* is

[5]The Biblioteca Nacional had been transferred, in 1826, to the former palace of the Duques de Algete, in what was consequently named the Calle de la Biblioteca; it is now known as the Calle de Arrieta.

[6]Cejador y Frauca (*op. cit.*, 238, 255), both in his text and his bibliography makes the mistake of giving the date of this work as 1837. This is absurd, since the Cortes were meeting in 1844—to discuss a reform of the constitution of 1837.

[7]The Cortes Reformadoras elaborated the Constitution of 1845, much more con-servative than that of 1837, which it replaced. Article 11 declared that *"La religión de la Nación española es la católica, apostólica y romana"* and that *"El Estado se obliga a mantener el culto y sus ministros"* thus restoring to the Church its official status. The power of the crown was increased by the creation of a Senate of life-members appointed by the King. The King was to be allowed to marry and to leave the country without the permission of the Cortes. Although Campoamor recognized the necessity of revising the Constitution of 1837, he opposed the reactionary character of the reform, particu-larly regarding the status of the Church.

[8]An edition of 1840 is mentioned by the *Enciclopedia Espasa-Calpe*, art. "Campoa-mor," bibliography, but it elsewhere gives the date as 1848 (p. 1312, col. 2). The editors of the *Obras completas* know of only one edition—that of 1846.

constantly imitated, beginning with the title itself. In this opuscule, Campoamor's liberalism appears in its most unalloyed state. This honor might be shared by the longer and more original work, *El personalismo* (1855).[9] In it, our poet-philosopher is spontaneous, alert, intelligent, liberal and Francophile. Alas! No subsequent book of his will deserve all these epithets without qualification.

Campoamor's conversion to more conservative views seems to have been the result of bitter experiences as a public administrator. From 1847 to 1854, Campoamor was Governor of three turbulent *Levante* provinces successively, firstly Castellón ·de la Plana, then Alicante, and finally Valencia itself. However, it was not so much the events during his administration as the Revolution of '54,[10] which put an end to it, that aroused the reactionary lurking in him. Soon after this crisis, in 1857, Campoamor published his essay *Bacon*,[11] which, as explained elsewhere, gives both a red and a white reaction to ideological litmuspaper.

It is to be feared, moreover, that Campoamor was desirous of establishing himself socially. This alone can explain his "Discurso en la Real Academia Española" (1862), in which he seems ready to sacrifice all his intellectual integrity in order to satisfy the Germanophile and Francophobe reactionaries of the Academy. This might appear unlikely in view of the anecdotes illustrating the flippancy with which the author of the *Humoradas* treated the august corporation. The members were expected to bring *papeletas* for the compilation of the dictionary. During one session, the President asked Campoamor if he had fulfilled this obligation. The poet replied, without any respect for conventions— *"Tengo yo cara de traer papeletas?"*. Our epicurean had the disrespectful habit of falling asleep during sessions. On one occasion, the President

---

[9]The *Enciclopedia Espasa-Calpe*, art. "Campoamor," and Cejador y Frauca (*loc. cit.*) give the date as 1850, but the editors of Campoamor's *Obras completas* know of no such edition. The first edition of *El personalismo. Apuntes para una filosofía*, in point of fact, was published at Madrid by the Imprenta y Estereotipia de M. Rivadeneyra, Salón del Prado, núm. 8., in 1855.

[10]*Vide* Ildefonso Bermejo, *Alzamiento popular de 1854, que comprende desde la cuestión de ferrocarriles hasta la entrada del Duque de la Victoria en Madrid, y disposiciones posteriores* (Madrid: Mellado, 1854).

Cristino Martos y Balbí, *La revolución de Julio en 1854* (Madrid: Colegio de Sordomudos, 1854).

Emile de Girardin, *Révolution d'Espagne (1854). L'ornière des révolutions* (Paris: Librairie Nouvelle, 1856).

Charles de Mazade, *Les révolutions de l'Espagne contemporaine; quinze ans d'histoire, 1854-1868 (Paris: Didier, 1868).*

[11]Cejador y Frauca does not mention this work, not even in his bibliography.

awoke him and bade him bring at least one *papeleta*. The offender protested, "*Estos quieren que yo lo haga todo*," and then reclined once more in the arms of Morpheus.[12] These anecdotes are possibly apocryphal; in any case, this bantering does not signify real disrespect for established institutions.

A final consideration is the influence on the poet's rather mercurial nature of the wife whom he loved dearly and faithfully: while Governor of Alicante, he married Da. Guillermina O'Gorman, of Irish extraction, who was naïvely and uncompromisingly Catholic. Several incidents are told to illustrate the concessions which he made in order not to hurt her religious feelings.

Whatever the explanation, Campoamor's thought, in this period, became stuffily traditionalist and uninteresting. *Lo Absoluto* (1865)[13] marks perhaps his nadir in this respect. Its lyrical passages are frankly ludicrous:

"Revélate, mi alma, verdadero y único pensamiento mío. . . . Rechaza, alma mía, con el noble ardor con que has sido creada y con la convicción que te presta el convencimiento de la existencia de lo absoluto creador, esa invasión de la barbarie psicológica. . . ." (I, 543-44).

The Franco-German War of 1870 provoked a revulsion in Campoamor and a temporary revival of his liberalism. It was in this spirit that he wrote the one-act dialogue *Guerra a la guerra* (1870). *El ideísmo* (1883) is a peculiar mixture of liberalism and conservatism. There is a distinctly liberal note in the poem *El Licenciado Torralba* (1888), but it cannot be regarded as fundamental, since the poem is a pastiche.[14] Surrounded by the reverence of the multitude and the deference of high society, the poet sank slowly back into his conservatism. Yet his traditionalism was never stereotyped, and those who analyzed his ideas were always suspicious as to their absolute orthodoxy. Manuel de la Revilla published

---

[12]Andrés González-Blanco, *Campoamor* (Madrid: Sáenz de Jubera Hermanos, 1911), 193.

[13]The question of the absolute is very complex. *Vide* H. B. Baillie, "Absolute," in Hasting's *Encyclopædia of Religion and Ethics*. However, for Campoamor, it was merely another aspect of his campaign on behalf of "metaphysics," as against positivism and empiricism.

[14]Campoamor invented the figure of Catalina and wove an amorous intrigue onto the legend of Eugenio Torralba, commonly known as El Licenciado Torralba, who was condemned in 1531, for nicromancy, by the Inquisition of Cuenca. The Royal Library at Madrid possesses a copy of Torralba's trial. Extracts from it have been published by Pellicer. *Vide* Diego Clemencín's edition of *Don Quijote* (Madrid: Viuda de Hernando, 1894), VII, 67ff., footnote.

in the *Revista Contemporánea* of February 28, 1877, a study of Campoamor in which he declared

> "Damas aristocráticas, que contribuyen al dinero de San Pedro y son enemigas del art. 11; gentes que se cuentan en el número de *personas sensatas que tienen que perder;* niñas románticas y llenas de ilusiones devoran con placer estas máximas que en otros labios les parecerían impiás, escandalosas y dignas de anatema."[15]

We must not stress unduly this revival of Campoamor's heterodoxy; throughout the latter half of his life, he was a traditionalist without being a literalist. When he died, an octogenarian, in 1901, he was, at his own request, buried in the habit of the Carmelite Order.[16]

---

[15]Revilla, of whom we shall hear more in discussing Krausism, justifies our choice of Campoamor as the object of one of these studies when he says:
"Campoamor es a la vez reflejo exacto de su época y de su país" (p. 530).

[16]Presumably Campoamor was wrapped in the dull white habit of the lay brothers. It is not clear whether Campoamor was connected with the subordinated Cofradía del Carmen, or Cofradía del Escapulario as it was popularly known, since the induction-ceremony consisted in the imposition of a scapulary by a Carmelite Father. This *confradía* was extremely popular at the time of Campoamor's death. The advantages of membership were most marked in the afterworld, for Pope John XXII had granted to the *cofradía* the *Bula Sabatina*, which promised its members a quick release from the pains of Purgatory.

CHAPTER II

The Elusive Metaphysics of Campoamor

THE critic who attempts to reduce Campoamor's metaphysics to a system is finally compelled to admit that even Minerva would need the help of her father in order to accomplish the task.[1] The chaos is produced by several circumstances. The fundamental difficulty is that Campoamor had little flair for consistency. Moreover, following the plan already analyzed, his ideas developed so unevenly that it is possible to detect flagrant contradictions in statements separated by only a short lapse of time. The problem is complicated because Campoamor, who is so prosaic in his poetry, attempts to enhance his prose by occasional lyrical passages, involved metaphors, weak witticisms, spiked insults and hollow aphorisms.

These exasperating defects arise from Campoamor's unphilosophical attitude toward philosophy. Instead of shutting himself up in an ivory tower, a kind of castle seldom found in Spain, he behaved like a politician conducting an electoral campaign. Nearly all his prose works were solos in the Wagnerian opera of some Spanish public controversy. This comparison is rather apt in view of the organization hidden behind some of these apparently improvised dramas. Such an arrangement is common in the Hispanic world. A well-known Latin-American writer once confessed to me that a polemic in which he had played a prominent part was the result of a secret arrangement. It was in this same way that Campoamor came to write *El personalismo*.[2] He tells us that he

---

[1] Menéndez y Pelayo, who disliked Campoamor, said of *El personalismo* and *Lo absoluto*, in his *Historia de los heterodoxos españoles* (ed. Miguel Artigas; Madrid: Victoriano Suárez, 1932):

"Su filosfía es humorismo puro, en que centellean algunas intuiciones felices, que demuestran que el espíritu del autor tenía alas para volar a las regiones ontológicas, si se hubiera sometido antes a la gimnasia dialéctica" (VII, 489).

It is unjust to describe Campoamor's philosophy as *"humorismo puro,"* even if by *humorismo* we understand *capriciousness*, unless by "philosophy" we mean metaphysics.

[2] Campoamor's use of the word *personalismo* is surprising. It constitutes one of the innumerable lacunae in the 1925 edition of the *Diccionario* of the Real Academia Española. Other dictionaries, including Roque Barcía, list the word, but consider it merely as an unusual synonym for *egoísmo*. Campoamor seems to have coined the word in the sense of the study of personality. This honor is generally accorded to Charles-Bernard Renouvier, who developed in his last period a philosophy which he put forward in a book entitled *Le personnalisme* (1902). It is curious that both Campoamor and Renouvier, without knowing each other, should invent this term.

was urged to publish the book by Berzosa,[3] Lorenzana,[4] Barca,[5] Castelar,[6] Canalejas,[7] Rayón,[8] Alzugaray,[9] Morayta,[10] and others:

[3]This is probably Antonio Berzosa, author of the plays *Hablar por boca de ganso* (1847) and *Quemar las naves* (1859).

[4]Presumably Juan Alvarez de Lorenzana (1818-1883), the journalist and politician who was Ministro de Estado when the Revolution of 1868 broke out. Together with Federico Balart he drew up the famous circular of October 4, intended to inform the European powers of the causes and intentions of the Revolution. His contributions to *El Diario Español* have been gathered together under the title *Lorenzana y su obra*.

[5]Francisco Barca Corral (1831-83): Famous in his day as an orator in the Ateneo, in the Academia de Jurisprudencia and in the Congreso. But, *verba volant*. Appointed Minister to the United States in 1881, he committed suicide two years later.

[6]*Vide* Andrés Sánchez del Real, *Emilio Castelar, su vida, su carácter, sus costumbres, sus obras, sus discursos, su influencia en la idea democrática* (Barcelona, 1873).

Miguel Boada y Balmes, *Emilio Castelar, o refutación de las teorías de este orador, y de los errores del credo democrático* (Valencia, 1874).

F. de Sandoval, *Emilio Castelar. Coup d'œil sur sa vie* (Paris, 1886).

David Hannay, *Don Emilio Castelar* (in "Public Men of Today" series; London, 1896).

Madame Rattazzi, *Une époque. Emilio Castelar. Sa vie, son œuvre, son rôle historique* (special number of *La Nouvelle Revue Internationale*; Paris, 1899).

Miguel Morayta, *Juventud de Castelar, su vida de estudiante y sus primeros pasos en la política* (Madrid, 1901). This work has naturally an especial interest for us.

Manuel González Araco, *Castelar; su vida y su muerte* (Madrid, 1901).

For several decades Campoamor had frequent but not too friendly relations with Castelar. All these works throw some light upon them. Castelar (born 1832) had, at the time of publication of *El personalismo* just left the University of Madrid, where he had obtained his doctorate with a thesis on *Lucano, su vida, su genio, su poema* (1853).

[7]Francisco de Paula Canalejas y Casas (1834-83), not to be confused with his more famous nephew, José Canalejas y Méndez (born 1854). Canalejas y Casas was professor of literature at the University of Madrid, author of a large number of literary studies, and a close friend of Emilio Castelar, in collaboration with whom he wrote the novel *Don Alfonso el Sabio*.

[8]Damián Menéndez de Rayón published in 1861 an anthology entitled *Pensamientos de Campoamor extractados de sus obras* and, in 1867, together with F. del Villar, a Spanish translation of Emile Fisco et J. van der Straeten's *Institutions et taxes locales de la Grande Bretagne et de l'Irlande* (Paris, 1863).

[9]The only remnant of the fame of Ricardo Alzugaray is a lecture he gave in 1863 at the Ateneo on "Del monopolio de la industria papelera y sus efectos." It is reproduced by Luis María Pastor, *Conferencias libre-cambistas. Discursos pronunciados en el Ateneo de Madrid* (1863).

[10]Miguel Morayta Sagrario (1834-1917); professor at the University of Madrid, took a prominent part in the Revolution of 1868, being secretary of the Junta Revolucionaria Madrileña. During the Restoration, he distinguished himself chiefly by his anti-clerical activities. He was president of the Liga Anticlerical. Having become Gran Maestre of the Gran Oriente Nacional de Espana, he united it with other Masonic societies to form the Gran Oriente Español. Like the other participants in the polemic concerning *El personalismo*, he was young at the time.

"El objeto que nos hemos propuesto personas de tan distintos caracteres y tan diferentes escuelas es el de que, publicada una obra original cualquiera sobre filosofía, diese lugar a una viva polémica; polémica que, sostenida por cada uno de nosotros desde el punto de vista de nuestras respectivas escuelas, produjese en el país el objeto contrario del que se proponía cierta universidad que el año de 1824 decía a Fernando VII: 'Señor, felicitamos a V.M. porque ha concluído con la fatal manía de pensar.' Francamente, con permiso de esta estulta universidad, desde la de *hacer tiempo* se se pueden reconocer en los españoles todas las manías imaginables, menos la de *pensar*. Voy yo pues a ser el hijo de Tell de esta polémica y me presento resignado con la manzana sobre la cabeza" (I, 365).

This system had unfortunate results. In *Polémicas con la democracia* (1862) and the related works, it cannot be gainsaid that Campoamor, on the one hand, and, on the other, Castelar and Canalejas are abusing each other without any pretense and with real bad feeling. The polemic about Krausism begun in 1875 between Campoamor and Canalejas was the result of another half-friendly agreement. Canalejas wrote:

"Discutiremos si lo cree usted oportuno. Usted decidirá" (III, 49).

The unfortunate result was a storm in the sea of Iberian spleen, which did not make for easy intellectual sailing. Nevertheless, although these polemics may have little intrinsic worth, they are invaluable documents about the intellectual life of the Spain of their time.

After such faint praise of Campoamor's intellectual methods, it may sound ironical to state that the key to Campoamor's thought is intelligence, which is the sole and absolute criterion on which he based his philosophy. Throughout *El personalismo*, he stresses intelligence to the exclusion of all other human qualities:

"En la especie humana todo lo que no es inteligente es una especie de sub-género" (I, 146).

In the poem "Lo que es eterno," dedicated to the Conde de San Luis on the occasion of the founding of the Teatro Español,[11] Campoamor proclaims that intelligence alone defeats time:

---

[11]The Teatro del Príncipe was destroyed by fire in 1804 and rebuilt according to designs by Villanueva. In 1849 it was restored and renamed Teatro Español. The Conde de San Luis wished to give it a public status similar to that of the Théâtre Français, but the proposal failed.

"Y es que la idea que en los cielos flota,
fija cual Dios, como de Dios esencia,
del tiempo móvil la guadaña embota
Por eso, al declinar de la existencia,
de entre las ruinas de los mundos brota,
crisálida inmortal, la inteligencia"   (V, 127).

The lines, which contain a chaos of metaphors, are not quoted on account of their artistic value, which is nil. That a Spaniard should proclaim intelligence paramount shows what repercussions French philosophy of the eighteenth century was producing in Iberia. It would be malicious to confess that this constant and undisguised eulogy of reason makes the reader suspect that Campoamor was decidedly proud of his own abilities.

Campoamor first applied his intelligence to the positivist sciences. There is a significant autobiographical passage in *El personalismo:*

"Casi todos los liberales españoles de provincia, educados por les libros de los sabios franceses del siglo pasado, profesan como artículo de fe la opinión de que no hay más ciencias dignas de estudio que las experimentales, ni más ciencias experimentales que las naturales, ni más ciencias naturales que las físicas. Impregnada mi familia de estas ideas empíricas, me mandó a la corte a estudiar medicina" (I, 271-72).

The phenomenon which Campoamor describes is well-known, but we cannot accept his application of it to himself. He had a rather cavalier attitude toward truth, as when, in answer to accusations that he plagiarized Victor Hugo, he affirmed that he could not even read French. Compoamor was already a well-established member of society when he published *El personalismo.* With obvious disgust, Castelar once implicitly accused him of showing little dignity in concealing his humble origin.[12] We fear that Campoamor was guilty of the same hypocrisy when he wrote the above passage. He was implying that his family belonged to the well-to-do nobility which had enjoyed cultural relations with France; for liberals were usually members of the aristocracy. In point of fact, as we have seen, Campoamor's family brought him up in such a traditionalist fashion that he almost became a Jesuit. If they gave him a small allowance in order that he might study in Madrid, it was so that he might earn a respectable living.

Whatever the truth be, Campoamor studied medicine for two years

---

[12] *Vide Polémicas con la democracia,* II, 438.

and came into contact with the positivist sciences. He describes, in *El personalismo*, how little satisfaction he found in these studies and how great was his disappointment. He devoted his attention for a while to botany but abandoned this study because it promised nothing beyond a detailed knowledge of the classification which Jussieu had established for the plant world (I, 273).[13] Chemistry likewise offered him little except the nomenclature formulated by Lavoisier;[14] names and classifications were all that Campoamor could see in any of the positivist sciences. For a time he studied mathematics with a certain Alejandro de Bengoechea but soon decided that mathematics has no use except to measure weight and distances; that it deals with things objective, accidental, and phenomenal (I, 274). Our encyclopedist also sampled zoology; he found himself confronted with the system of Cuvier, which he felt he could learn but never hope to improve (I, 274-75).[15] As a last resort, he tried astronomy:[16]

---

[13]The first classification of the plant world was established by Carl von Linné (1707-78), i.e. Linnæus, in his *Genera plantarum* (1737), *Classes plantarum* (1738), and *Species plantarum* (1753). Linnæus' work was so well known in Spain that in 1755, Fernando VI invited him to settle in the peninsula, with a good remuneration and free from the Inquisition. But Linnæus declined, saying that he wished to devote himself to the service of Sweden, and sent Löfling instead. The Jussieu family devoted itself with singular unanimity to botany, the most outstanding representatives being the three brothers Antoine de Jussieu (1686-1758), Bernard de Jussieu (1699-1777), Joseph de Jussieu (1704-1779), their nephew Antoine-Laurent de Jussieu (1748-1836) and the latter's son, Adrien de Jussieu (1797-1853). *Vide* Marie Jean Pierre Flourens, *The Jussieus and the Natural Method* (Washington: Smithsonian Institution, 1867). Campoamor is referring to Antoine-Laurent de Jussieu, who revised the artificial classification of Linnæus in his *Genera plantarum secundum ordines naturales disposita* (1788). Probably Campoamor studied botany under the then famous botanist Vicente Cutanda (died 1866), who was a member of the commission appointed to make a geological map of the province of Madrid. In relation with this project, Vicente Cutanda published *Flora compendiada de Madrid y de su provincia* (1861). He was Jardinero Mayor of the Jardín Botánico, and as such published, in collaboration with Alonso y Quintanilla and Pascual Asensio, a *Catálogo* of the garden (1849) and a *Catálogo adicional* (1850). Together with Mariano del Amo he wrote a once-standard *Manual de botánica descriptiva* (1848).

[14]*Vide* Douglas McKie, *Antoine Lavoisier* (Philadelphia: J. B. Lippincott, 1935), chap. viii. Guyton de Morveau led the movement toward an improved chemical nomenclature; in 1782, Lavoisier, Berthollet and Fourcroy began collaborating with him in devising a new system. The four published their *Méthode de nomenclature chimique* at Paris in 1787. Lavoisier produced two years later his still more important *Traité élémentaire de chimie*. Whereas Lavoisier recognized and named thirty-three elements, Fermi has just brought the total to ninety-three.

[15]*Vide* Louis Roule, *Cuvier et la science de la nature* (Paris: Flammarion, 1926). Of the works of Baron Georges-Léopold-Chrétien-Frédéric-Dagobert Cuvier (1769-1832),

"Desencantado de las mecánicas terrestres, volví los ojos al cielo. . . . Pero; ay! esos inmensos átomos, llamados soles, no sólo no sirven para resolver el problema de la Divinidad, sino que no se puede descubrir con ellos ni siquiera la X atracción" (I, 275).

In other words, Campoamor proclaimed, long before Brunetière, "la banqueroute de la science." His scornful conclusion is that:

"El estudio de las ciencias naturales es un oficio digno de figurar entre las artes mecánicas, entre las zapaterías, por ejemplo" (I, 277).

This typically Spanish attitude is a foretaste of Unamuno's attacks on el cientifismo.[17] Campoamor's criticisms are unjust and superficial. He is seeking, apparently, a means of rapidly ascertaining the metaphysical nature of the cosmos. He fails to see that the positivist sciences provide a slow but sure method of discovering the mechanism of the universe. They do not tell us the why, but they certainly reveal the how and can provide much more than mere nomenclature and classification.

Besides this general criticism of the positivist sciences, Campoamor has penned a number of more developed attacks on some of these disciplines. In the same work, El personalismo (1855), which appeared four years before Darwin's Origin of the Species (1859), there is to be found a tirade, which today sounds quaint, against the supporters of the theory of evolution:[18]

"¡Naturalistas! ¡Reclutas de Manés! ¡Calumniadores del género humano, que aunque no lo decís claramente, sé yo que opináis que Adán ha sido hijo o por lo menos nieto de un mono! No os quiero

Campoamor is doubtless referring to Le règne animal distribué d'après son organisation (1816-29). Cuvier devoted his energies to a rather arid classification of existing forms. Had Campoamor turned to the other heir of Buffon, namely Jean-Baptiste-Pierre-Antoine de Monet, Chevalier de Lamarck, and read his Philosophie zoologique (1809), or his Histoire des animaux sans vertèbres (1815-22), he would have found a much more fruitful vision of zoology, in which the time element is considered. However, Campoamor would probably have condemned his evolutionary ideas.

[16]For the state of astronomy at that time, vide Hector Macpherson, Makers of Astronomy (Oxford: Clarendon Press, 1933). Probably, Campoamor was much more influenced by the Mécanique céleste (1799-1825) and the Exposition du système du monde (1796-1824) of Pierre Simon Laplace than by the less accessible writings of William Herschel.

[17]Vide Ronald Hilton, "Unamuno, Spain, and the World," Bulletin of Spanish Studies, XIV (1937), 66-67.

[18]Probably Campoamor was thinking of Buffon and his colleague Dauberton, who, in order to prove man's relationship with the animal world, devoted careful attention to monkeys. Vide Dauberton La situation du trou occipital dans l'homme et dans les animaux (1764).

agobiar en este mundo con el peso de mis maldiciones, porque tengo presente el terrible castigo que Manés, filósofo persa, os impone después de muertos. ¡Es una horrible historia! !Cuenta Manés que e mundo, la materia, vuestra querida la materia, existirá siempre; pero es el caso que, a la consumación de los siglos, quedará reducida a un estado cadavérico y todas las almas que, como las de vosotros los naturalistas, hayan seguido sus inspiraciones serán condenados a permanecer siempre silenciosas y tristes, haciendo la guardia a este cadáver eterno! ¡Naturalistas! ¡Reclutas de Manés! ¡Dios os dé paciencia en vuestra futura centinela!" (I, 278).[19]

Campoamor was equally hostile to the materialistic psychology, propounded chiefly by doctors, which left no place for the soul. The exponent in Spain of these theories, reminiscent of Claude Bernard, was Pedro Mata, author of a *Tratado de la razón humana*.[20] Campoamor devotes the whole of Artículo XXV ("*artículo*" is the equivalent of section) of *Polémicas con la democracia* to the refutation of this "philosophy."

---

[19]At the time, the standard work on this subject was the voluminous *Histoire de Manichée et du Manichéisme* (2 vols; Amsterdam: Frederic Bernard, 1734-39) of M. de Beausobre. However, it does not contain the story related by Campoamor, who is misinformed. According to Manichaeism, at the end of time, all matter will be precipitated into Hell and will burn like an immense cauldron. Inveterate sinners will accompany it in this process. *Vide* P. Alfaric, *L'evolution intellectuelle de Saint Augustin*, Part I, Sect. I, chap. iii, and A. V. Williams Jackson, *Researches in Manichaeism* (New York: Columbia University Press, 1933), p. 16. Campoamor seems to be confused with Mani's view of the world as it is. *Vide* Prosper Alfaric, *Les écritures manichéennes* (Paris: Emile Noudry, 1918):

"D'après Mani, certains Archontes ténébreux avaient été tués et écorchés par le Démiurge. Tandis que leurs peaux habilement tendues avaient formé le firmament, leurs chairs constituaient la terre et leurs os les montagnes. De leur chevelure était nés les légumes et de leur fiel était sorti le vin. D'autre part le Démiurge s'était donné cinq fils qui lui servaient d'auxiliaires et dout chacun veillait avec lui sur la terre" (p. 38). Incidentally, Manichaeism has a long and important tradition in Spain. *Vide* Alfaric, pp. 62ff.

[20]More precisely, of a series of books on the subject: *Filosofía española. Tratado de la razón humana con aplicación a la práctica del foro* (Madrid, 1858), *Filosofía española. Tratado de la razón humana en sus estados intermedios* (Madrid, 1864). *Tratado de la razón humana en estado de salud* (Madrid, 1878), *Tratado de la razón humana en estado de enfermedad* (Madrid, 1878). Campoamor had, in his reactionary period, good reason for disliking Pedro Mata y Fontanet (1811-1877), a Catalan of advanced political ideas. In 1835, Mata founded *El Propagador de la Libertad*. In 1837, he took part in riots and was obliged to escape to Marseilles on board a warship. He returned to Reus in 1838 and founded *La Joven España*, but was imprisoned and once more exiled. In his latter years, he devoted himself chiefly to scientific research but was still widely

In his reactionary period, the Turk's head of Campoamor was the rapidly developing science of economics.[21] He regarded economists as dangerous dreamers who wished to tamper with the social order which, if left to Mother Nature, would take care of itself. This represents in reality a laissez-faire attitude. It was therefore stupid of Campoamor to criticize the exponents of this theory. When his fellow-Asturians proposed to raise a monument to the then-famous economist Flórez Estrada, Campoamor declared, with ill-concealed irritation, that every reference to property in his book was radically false and utterly revolutionary.[22] Adopting a tone of paternal despair, he exhorts those who have gone astray:

"¡Economistas inexpertos, a quienes amo con toda la sinceridad que me inspiran las aspiraciones generosas! dejad a los Smith,[23] Buchanan,[24] Ricardo,[25] Say,[26] etc., etc., a esos escritores sin arte, estadistas empíricos, filósofos de efectos sin causas, y elevándoos a las regiones de la Psicología, estudiad las categorías del entendimiento humano, donde hallaréis la regla de toda moral, de todo derecho, de toda libertad" (II, 582-83).

branded as anti-religious and materialistic. *Vide* Luis Comenge y Ferrer, *La medicina en el siglo xix* (Barcelona, 1914).

[21] *Vide* John Kells Ingram, *A History of Political Economy* (London: Black, 1915). O. Fred Boucke, *The Development of Economics, 1750-1900* (New York: Macmillan, 1921). G. H. Busquet, *Essai sur l'évolution de la pensée économique* (Paris: Marcel Giard, 1927).

[22] *Polémicas con la democracia*, II, 579. Alvaro Flórez Estrada was born at Pola de Somiedo (Asturias) in 1769 and died in 1853. He was a declared follower of Ricardo, McCulloch, and J. S. Mill. His most famous work is his *Curso de economía política* (1828), which went into a large number of editions, appearing at Madrid, Paris, or London; in some cases, the word *Curso* was replaced by *Tratado*. Flórez Estrada was a socialist in that he strove to improve the conditions of the lower classes, and Campoamor scarcely does himself credit by his angry opposition.

[23] Adam Smith (1739-1790).

[24] David Buchanan (1779-1848) published an annotated edition of Adam Smith's *Wealth of the Nations*, with a supplementary volume entitled *Observations on the Subjects Treated of in Dr. Smith's Inquiry* (Edinburgh, 1814). Buchanan criticized especially Adam Smith's rent theory and demanded a system of taxation which would not impose a hardship upon the recipients of small incomes.

[25] David Ricardo (1772-1823): *Works of David Ricardo* (ed. J. R. McCulloch; London, 1846). *Vide* J. H. Hollander, *David Ricardo; a Centenary Estimate* (Baltimore, 1910). Ricardo is usually regarded as the inspirer of the nineteenth century socialistic economists, including Rodbertus and Marx.

[26] Jean-Baptiste Say (1767-1832), above all an interpreter of Adam Smith; *Traité d'économie politique* (1803), *Cours complet d'économie politique pratique* (1828-29). *Vide* Ernest Teilhac, *L'œuvre économique de Jean-Baptiste Say* (1927).

Campoamor is evidently a conservative afraid of militant *intelectuales*. He applauds the study of things not connected with the *status quo* of society, but woe betide any intellectual who questions the validity of the economic structure of mankind!

Having demonstrated the uselessness of the positivist sciences, Campoamor attempts to vindicate philosophy against the attacks of positivist thinkers:

"Es menester vengar a la filosofía, a la ciencia del espíritu, que es la personalidad, que es la verdad, contra las diatribas de los *naturalistas*, que no son más que los obreros del arte de la materia, que es una objetividad pasajera, que es una mentira."

In 1862, Campoamor was elected to the Real Academia Española and, as for his *discurso de entrada*, chose the subject "La metafísica limpia, fija y da esplandor al lenguaje"—a parody of the Academy's motto. This unctuous address contained the first strong manifestation of the quasi-monomania which held Campoamor's mind in his reactionary period: the defense of metaphysics:

"¡Gloria a la metafísica, nuestra divina madre intelectual, en cuyo seno se engendran todos nuestros grandes pensamientos! Tronco de una posteridad eterna, la metafísica da a las ideas una vitalidad imperecedera, y todos los hijos que ella no engendra son engendros" (I, 394).[27]

Juan Valera, who had until then been favorably disposed toward Campoamor,[28] listened with amused interest to the address of the new academician and two days later, March 11, 1862, published in *El Contemporáneo*, of which he was editor, a long commentary, in which irony was coated with admiration:

"Envíele [el discurso] el Sr. de Campoamor a Alemania, donde le auguramos que ha de tener un éxito asombroso. Aquellos sabios, tan serios y tan de buena fe, tomarán por lo serio todas las sutilezas, discreteos y fantasías del Sr. de Campoamor, que es amigo de broma, y no faltarán entre ellos algunos que le sigan y que formen escuela o secta de sus doctrinas ultra-espiritualistas."[29]

The conservative priest Francisco Mateos Gago, famous at the time as

---

[27]*Engendrar* is a neutral word, whereas its pejorative deritive *engendro* is defined in the *Diccionario* of the Academy as: "Feto. Criatura que nace sin la proporción debida. Plan, designio u obra intelectual mal concebidos."

[28]*Vide* "Obras poéticas de Campoamor," *Obras completas*, XIX, 153ff.

[29]*Obras completas*, xxii, 85.

an apologist of Catholicism and an enemy of anticlericals such as Castle-lar, wrote a reply, defending metaphysical Campoamor, which Valera, with his usual tolerance, published in *El Contemporáneo*. However, he countered it, a day or two later, with a defense of his own position. The situation became complicated when, in the same year, 1862, shortly after Campoamor, Valera was elected to the Academy. His *discurso de entrada*, read on March 16, 1862, was meant to be a reply to that of Campoamor. It was entitled:

"La poesía popular como ejemplo del punto en que debieran coincidir la idea vulgar y la idea académica sobre la lengua castellana."[30]

Valera continued to deny the salutary effects of metaphysics on language. The result was a bitter controversy between the philosophical partisans of Campoamor and the positivist friends of Valera. We leave the details of this polemic for a future study of the Andalusian enemy of Asturian mystifications.

Even after a careful perusal of the musings of Campoamor, it is almost impossible to say what he understands by "metaphysics," since, at the same time that he condemns positivism, he attacks with equal animus the exponents of traditional philosophy. He seems to advocate what would now be called pragmatism: in *El personalismo*, he asserts:

"Yo clasifico a los filósofos, no por sus principios *teóricos*, sino por sus resultados *prácticos*" (I, 24).

He avers that, ever since its rebirth under Descartes, philosophy has lost itself in a useless pursuit of the origin of phenomena, rather than seeking their destination. He says, in blunt language, that he under-stands the general attitude toward philosophers, who are regarded as madmen running loose. Philosophy, he proceeds, has until now been nothing more than a form of insanity, which has not even been funny; it has been merely one three-century long headache. Feeling that this is a weak statement, Campoamor continues, multiplying the lapse of time by ten:

"Hace más de tres mil años que los fautores de filosofías están inquiriendo *causas* en vez de apoderarse de *los efectos* y descuidando lo real por buscarse lo imaginario, han convertido la filosofía en una química de abstracciones" (I, 20-21).

A few pages later, he explains his attitude more clearly:

"No busquéis los *noumenos*, es decir, no tratéis de penetrar la esencia

---

[30]*Obras completas*, I, 1ff.

de las cosas como *son en sí*, sino estudiad los *fenómenos*, esto es, el modo como se suceden las cosas. En la creación no importa tanto el *cómo* y el *cuándo*, cuanto el *por qué* y el *para qué*. Dejad la *causa*, vamos al *hecho*. No busquemos lo absolutamente esencial, sino lo absolutamente fenomenal'' (I, 23).

Except perhaps for the use of the word *absolutamente*, this passage could have been penned by a positivist. The essential difference seems to be that, while both opposed any abandonment of reality, the positivists stressed scientific disciplines, whereas Campoamor demanded a more human interpretation of phenomena, with some consideration of the hopes and aspirations of man.

Campoamor's interest in the fate of mankind is shown in the passages where he, the merciless enemy of positivism, praises materialism because, in drawing attention to this world, it has bettered the lot of mankind:

"La secta materialista es la rama de la filosofía que ha hecho más servicios en favor de la felicidad del género humano: ella inauguró el espíritu de indisciplina contra las chocheces dogmáticas de la vieja Sorbona, fué la pólvora que volólos aportillados muros del feudalismo y, por último, creó *el sentido común humano*'' (I, 28).

Sometimes Campoamor expresses a love of matter which sounds strange in the mouth of a defender of metaphysics:

"Eterna gratitud a la materia, a ese argumento tangible de la realidad de nuestro ser, de la existencia de nuestra personalidad'' (I, 63).

All this does not mean that he would have any philosophical truck with the materialist school, which he had more reason to dislike than that of the positivists:

"Yo no quiero que el pensar sea la *digestión de las impresiones* de Cabanis y que mis ideas, por consecuencia, sean una secreción orgánica del cerebro'' (I, 31).[31]

If Campoamor did not lash materialism with the merciless strictures inflicted on positivism, it was, no doubt, because he considered the

---

[31]Campoamor is referring to the famous sentence of Pierre-Jean-Georges Cabanis (1757-1808) in his *Rapports du physique et du moral de l'homme* (1802; 8th edit., probably the one used by Campoamor, Paris: Braillière, 1844). In the Second Mémoire, "Histoire physiologique des sensations," Cabanis compares thought with the physiological processes and asserts:

"Nous concluons que le cerveau digère en quelque sorte les impressions; qu'il fait organiquement la sécrétion de la pensée'' (p. 138).

former a historical philosophy whereas the latter was a burning question in his time.

Campoamor saw dangerous villains lurking on the righthand side of the narrow gate to truth, just as he denounced various positivistic sciences on the other side. It is significant to note that our Spaniard was especially untiring in his attacks on theology. In *El personalismo*, he says typically:

"Los Padres de la Iglesia han hablado tanto del alma, acabando, después de todo, por probar que ellos mismos no saben lo que es" (I, 249).

During his reactionary period, Campoamor sometimes paid lip-service to theology, as when, in *Lo absoluto*, he affirmed:

"Mi deseo hubiera sido poder imitar a Santo Tomás en el *modo de pensar* y a Espinosa en la *manera de exponer*. Estos dos filósofos son la delicia de mis lecturas: el primero por lo hondo y penetrante y el segundo por lo sintético y lo lógico" (I, 424).

In his more sincere moods, Campoamor declared his hatred of Spinoza, whom he considered as the originator of German philosophical mystifications. Our turn-coat was equally hypocritical in affirming his affection for Saint Thomas Aquinas. In his franker moments, he still continued to assert his cordial dislike of the theological saint.

In what is commonly denominated metaphysics, Campoamor had four pet hatreds. The first was æsthetics:

"Se ha creado una ciencia de la sensibilidad llamada *estética*, tan ilusoria en sus principios como estéril en sus resultados; hablo de la *estética* que se ha dado en llamar transcendental y que tiene por base la sensibilidad pura, una especie de aptitud o *potencia* de recibir representaciones" (I, 182).[32]

With regard to the intellectual history of nineteenth century Spain, it is interesting to note the reference in this passage to the words *estética* and *transcendental*, which seem to have been neologisms, and which, in subsequent literary polemics, were frequently used with decided self-consciousness.

Second on Campoamor's black list was psychology, by which must naturally be understood the abstract psychology of the classical philosophers:

---

[32]For a discussion of this complicated problem in the history of philosophy, *vide* Bernard Bosanquet, *A History of Æsthetic* (London: Swan Sonnenschein, 1892).

"Después de la *estética a priori* de las escuelas. . . . no es posible inventar una cosa más estéril que la *psicología pura*" (I, 202).[33]

This remark occurs in Book V of *El personalismo*, which is entitled "Del hombre considerado individualmente." Campoamor there discusses the various characteristics of man in a homely fashion reminiscent of moral theologians.

Third and fourth in the infernal quartet are transcendental logic and pure ideology. After an unsympathetic analysis of the ideas of Descartes and Kant, Campoamor says in disgust:

"Después de la *estética* transcendental y de la *psicología* pura de las escuelas, no es posible inventar una cosa más estéril que esta lógica *transcendental* y esta *ideología pura*" (I, 234-35).

It is evident, then, that, throughout his life, Campoamor edged gingerly or strutted recklessly up and down a tight-rope, struggling not to fall into positivism on the one hand or transcendentalism on the other. If it pleased him to call this tight-rope "metaphysics," it was an abuse of terms and a dangerous one, since it involved him in a number of polemics which seem to have arisen chiefly through an excessive stress on terminology. In constantly uttering the word *metafísica* as a trumpet-call, Campoamor was actively taking sides in the polemic, Positivism versus Metaphysics, which was raging throughout Europe at the time.[34] Had he really understood the issue, Campoamor might equally well have proclaimed a crusade in defense of positivism. He was probably swayed, as a poet, by the fact that a number of philosophers, notably Lange and Renan, were describing metaphysics as "the poetry of the ideal."

The principal of the resultant controversies took place inside the Ateneo, the two protagonists being Cánovas del Castillo, at the time the respected President of that liberal and intellectual association, and Campoamor, President of its literary section. Cánovas del Castillo, who was a mild positivist,[35] said in a speech:

---

[33] Kant had affirmed that psychology cannot be subjected to mathematical discipline and therefore cannot be a science. Johann F. Herbart, in his *Lehrbuch zur Psychologie* (1816) attempted to refute this and to make psychology a mathematical science. Campoamor was apparently protesting against the school of psychologists following Herbart.

[34] *Vide* Alfred Fouillée, *L'avenir de la métaphysique* (Paris: Félix Alcan, 1890).

[35] On the philosophical ideas of Cánovas del Castillo, *vide* Adolfo Pons y Umbert, *Cánovas del Castillo* (Madrid: Hernández, 1901), chap. iv. On Cánovas in the Ateneo, *vide* El Marqués de Lema, *Cánovas o el hombre de estado* (in "Vidas españolas e hispanoamericanas del siglo xix"; Madrid: Espasa-Calpe, 1931), pp. 83-84. Despite this con-

"La verdadera filosofía parece como que al presente duerme, rendido el cuerpo a la fatiga. Mientras no aparezcan nuevas direcciones que den siquiera remota esperanza de llegar más lejos, o de subir más arriba, conviene ahora hacer alto y esperar por algún tiempo, hasta que naturalmente recobre la metafísica su imperio y despierte el pensamiento filosófico con nuevo brío, dedicando nuestra actividad en el interim a otros ramos del saber" (III, 415).

In the Introduction to *El ideísmo* (1883),[36] Campoamor protests hotly and retorts:

"¿Pero es que el señor Cánovas del Castillo cree que puede existir ningún ramo del saber del cual no constituya la parte más principal la metafísica?" (id).

The reader finds it impossible to say what this sentence means, or what connotation Campoamor gives to the word *metafísica*. It sounds suspiciously like a parrot-cry. Campoamor proceeds to express regret that the Ateneo should allow itself to be dragged along in the positivist current:

"¿Le parece que a esta brillante juventud del Ateneo la debemos dejar que siga viviendo intelectualmente en compañía de esos sabios de temporada, llamados Comte, Moleschot [*sic*],[37] Bernard, Büchner,[38] Spencer y otros?" (III, 416).

Campoamor made a desperate attempt to rekindle in the Ateneo the

---

troversy, Campoamor remained a close friend of Cánovas, of whom he published a biography entitled *Cánovas, estudio biográfico* (In series "Personajes ilustres," Madrid, n.d., pp. 43).

[36]Both the *Espasa* (art. "Campoamor") and Cejador y Frauca (VII, 255) distort this title into *El idealismo*, through confusion probably with *El personalismo*. Campoamor was determined to establish himself as a philosopher by using his own terminology; just as he preceded Renouvier in inventing *personalismo* as a philosophical term, so he created the word "*ideísmo*," which is not recognized either by the Academy or by Roque Barcía. Each of the chapter titles of *El ideísmo* contains the words "*las ideas.*" From *idea*, Campoamor derived *ideísmo*, as opposed to *idealismo*, from *ideal*.

[37]Jacob Moleschott (1822-1893): A Dutch naturalist, professor of physiology at Heidelberg, and later, after his materialist opinions had made him flee Germany, at Rome.

[38]Undoubtedly Ludwig Büchner (1824-1899), less known than his literary brother Georg. He was a materialist and a follower of Darwin. His ideas became widely known through his once-famous book *Kraft und Stoff* (1855). He published also *Natur und Geist* (1857), *Physiologishe Bilder* (1861-1875), *Die Darwinsche Theorie von der Entstehung und Umwandlung der Lebewelt* (1868), *Der Gottesbegriff und dessen Bedeutung in der Gegenwort* (1874), *Am Sterbelager des Jahrhunderts* (1898), *Im Dienste der Wahrheit* (1899).

flame of *la metafísica*. When he was elected President of the *sección de literatura*, he proposed, *"venciendo mi natural indiferencia hacia casi todas las cosas de este mundo"* (why these melodramatic phrases?), that the section discuss this theme:

"De las ideas representadas por los grandes hombres en la filosofía, en la historia y en el arte."

He had the support of his secretaries, Abelardo Ortiz de Pinedo[39] and José Acevedo,[40] but many considered the subject *"vago, incomprensible y extraño."* Campoamor succeeded in making them revise their opinion, and a long symposium ensued. The poet's vindictiveness was appeased:

"Desde el mismo día en que se efectuó la primera de nuestras discusiones, ya pude dar una buena noticia al señor Cánovas del Castillo, y es que, mientras que él arriaba por algún tiempo la bandera de la metafísica, los socios de la sección de literatura, hasta los de color rojo más subido, la desplegaban al aire gloriosamente" (III, 425).

The debate began with a *memoria* by the first secretary, Abelardo Ortiz de Pinedo, who appealed to the ideal of right. He was followed by Juan Martos Jiménez, who exhorted his friends to put their democratic ideas on a metaphysical basis. Of the next speaker José Zahonero,[41] Campoamor tells us that:

"Al fijar los ojos del cuerpo en las realidades de aquí abajo, se le escapaban miradas de los ojos del alma hacia un idealismo que reconocía como un hecho *incontrovertible"* (id).

The platform was successively adorned by José Rodríguez Carracido,[42]

---

[39]The Ortiz de Pinedo family was not without distinction in nineteenth century Spanish cultural life (cf. Domingo O. de P., Fabián O. de P., José O. de P., Manuel O. de P., and Manuel O. de P., son). However, Abelardo has left practically no trace.

[40]This is apparently José María Fernández de la Puente y Acevedo, who wrote a *Memoria sobre que la arqueología es la base de las ciencias, de las artes y del comercio* (Madrid: 1854).

[41]José Zahonero (1853-1931) took part in the revolutionary events of 1874 and was forced to flee to France. He soon returned to Spain and was connected with several newspapers. However, he became better known as a writer of short stories. As a novelist, he followed Zola closely and defended naturalism in a series of polemics. One of his first novels, *La carnaza* (1885), won for him a foremost place among Spanish naturalists. He was later converted to Catholicism.

[42]José Rodríguez Carracido (1856-1928), was a famous professor of medicine at the University of Madrid. He was also Rector of the University, a member of the Academia Española, and a Senator. In 1898, in the columns of *El Imparcial*, he engaged with Cardenal González in a polemic about *"el darwinismo transformista."* His two best-known works are a *Tratado de química orgánica* and a *Tratado de química biológica*, of which a large number of editions appeared.

Julio Burrell,[43] Fernando Soldevilla,[44] Lorenzo Benito,[45] who differed in their religious and philosophical ideas, but all shared an enthusiastic cult of art. They were succeeded by Urbano González Serrano,[46] who revealed his love of compromise by declaring that, within the positivist doctrines he upheld, there palpitated something mysteriously metaphysical. Ignacio Pintado,[47] Conrado Solsona[48] and Miguel Sánchez[49] also took part in the discussions (III, 426). Campoamor was a great admirer of the last-named, a then-famous ecclesiastic. The exact relationship between these various addresses and the topic under discussion is not clear, nor how they contributed to restore metaphysics

---

[43]For Julio Burrell, vide Ronald Hilton, Pardo-Bazán, Spain, and the World.

[44]Fernando Soldevilla Ruiz (1854-1931): Born of peasant family, he himself worked in the fields until he was sixteen years old. He came to Madrid, entered journalism, founded La Linterna, was exiled on account of an article which appeared in it, and, returning after a two years sojourn in Paris, became a respected member of Madrid society. He is best known on account of the yearly publication El Año Político, which he founded in 1895, and which gave a summary, day by day, of political affairs in Spain and abroad.

[45]Lorenzo Benito de Endara (born 1855), a professor of Mercantile law, at Valencia, Barcelona, and Madrid successively. He published a large number of works on his speciality.

[46]As the principal editor of the Obras completas of Campoamor, which form the nucleus for this study, Urbano González Serrano (1848-1904) has for us an especial interest. He studied philosophy with Nicolás Salmerón and taught it at the Instituto de San Isidro. Politically a radical, he never accepted the Restoration, and in 1881 he became a Republican deputy. He represented the second phase of Krausism, in which the pantheistic system was abandoned in favor of scientific neo-positivism. A friend of Giner de los Ríos, he was closely connected with the Institución Libre de Enseñanza. From his pen came almost all the articles on philosophy and philosophers in the Diccionario enciclopédico hispano-americano. He was a close friend of Revilla, who was a protagonist in the polemic concerning Krausism which we discuss elsewhere; in collaboration with Revilla, González Serrano published Elementos de ética o filosofía moral (Madrid, 1874). He composed a considerable number of other philosophical treatises, always written from the Krausist standpoint.

[47]Ignacio Pintado y Llorca has left little trace except for his Observaciones filosóficas sobre las causas del communismo (Valencia, 1874).

[48]Conrado Solsona (1851-1916): A journalist and a politician, Solsona was deputy, senator, and governor, yet found time to write a number of books. The most interesting from our viewpoint is El humorismo (1887).

[49]It is significant that a portrait of this liberal and intellectual prelate (died 1889), by M. Rouzé, hangs on the walls of the Ateneo, where he defended staunchly the traditionalist standpoint. At first, he was an ardent Carlist, expressing his ideas in La Regeneración and La Lealtad of which he was editor. Later he became reconciled with the Restoration, and conducted from the columns of El Tiempo a vigorous campaign against the uncompromising Siglo Futuro.

to its erstwhile prestige. In any case, Campoamor thought that he had got the better of Cánovas del Castillo in this guerrilla warfare.

Besides this battle between two armies, a duel resulted from Campoamor's exaltation of *la metafísica*. Since their first scuffle, already discussed, Valera had definitely adopted the positivist standpoint and condemned as useless both metaphysics and poetry. This gave rise to two polemics between the famous authors. The first came in 1865, three years after the exchange of salvoes in the Academy: Valera, in the March and April numbers of his newspaper *El Contemporáneo*, published a series of articles commenting unfavorably on *Lo Absoluto*.[50] A quarter of a century later, the two once more engaged in a controversy. The contributions of both were collected and published in book form under the title *La metafísica y la poesía, polémica, por don Ramón de Campoamor y don Juan Valera* (Madrid: Sáenz de Jubera Hermanos, 1891). The articles by Campoamor are to be found in Vol. III of his *Obras completas*, where they are gathered under the heading *La metafísica y la poesía ante la ciencia moderna*. The arguments of the poet-metaphysician are very flimsy. This controversy is discussed later in connection with Campoamor's ideas on poetry.

In the course of this altercation, Campoamor attacked Macaulay, who had been praised by Valera for having, in his essay on Bacon,[51] proclaimed the uselessness of speculative philosophy:

"¿Y con qué derecho se tomaba Macaulay esos aires de autoridad científica? Con ninguno. Como él despreciaba la metafísica, y no escribió ningún sistema de filosofía, se quedó siendo un crítico a la buena de Dios, que acertó en algunos juicios por casualidad, como todo el que se deja guiar sólo por su instinto y no por la ciencia" (III, 389).

The frail critic, weary of long wanderings in the labyrinth of these polemics, feels his benevolence failing and his mind suggesting that Campoamor the philosopher has here painted an excellent self-portrait.

---

[50]"Cartas al Sr D. Ramón de Campoamor sobre su libro de 'Lo absoluto'" *Obras completas*, xxxv, 11ff.

[51]"Lord Bacon," *Complete Works of Thomas Babington Macaulay* (Boston: Houghton Mifflin, 1900) *Critical and Historical Essays*, II, 357ff. This long study originally appeared in the *Edinburgh Review* of June, 1837.

CHAPTER III

THE RELIGION OF CAMPOAMOR

(i) *The Religious Urge*

ALTHOUGH, following the example of the *philosophes*, Campoamor exalted intelligence and reason, the Iberian tradition was strong enough in him to prevent his proclaiming their omnipotence and attempting, with their aid, to evolve a religion. Like most of his fellow-countrymen, even of the liberal stamp, our poet recognized the limits of reason:

"La razón aislada es la araña de nuestra naturaleza, que fabrica telas de su propia substancia, que vive de roerse a sí misma y que, girando abrazada a un fantasma que le sirve de eje, se atonta dando vueltas como si estuviese ebrio."[1]

Only the heart, says our poet, can guide man through the spiritual world. With the florid rhetoric of his time, Campoamor bids us:

"Discurramos con la mano puesta sobre el corazón" (I, 30). This does not mean that Campoamor abandons his intellectual criterion. Reason must always prevail, but it can only explore the higher regions of sentiment when sustained by emotion:

"Yo bendigo la razón, pero la razón lanzada hasta Dios por el proyectil del sentimiento" (I, 31).

This concept of a vital intellect in a way precedes the philosophy of Ortega y Gasset.

The keynote to Campoamor's religious musings is Iberian *Yo*. *Yo* is the be-all and the end-all not only here, but throughout eternity. *Yo* is the focus of the universe:

"La naturaleza es el gran laboratorio del Yo" (I, 54).

This remark could have been made by Unamuno.[2]

The great enemy of the *Yo* is mortality. True to the Spanish tradition, despite his French affiliations, Campoamor affirms that the fundamental fact of life is death. To this idea he devotes the chapter "Amor a la vida" of *El personalismo:*

"El árbol de la verdadera ciencia radica en la tumba. . . . La muerte, crisol de la immortalidad, plena posesión de lo que hay en nosotros

---

[1]*El personalismo*, I, 30.

[2]Campoamor is probably influenced in this cult of the *Yo* by his enemy Fichte, who exalted the *Ich. Vide* Maria Raich, *Fichte* (Tubigen, 1905), Zweiter Teil, "Fichtes Stellung zum Problem des Individualismus."

26

de más íntimo, de más personal, es el objeto más espantable para los seres que raciocinan. . . . El horror a nuestra destrucción es la idea primordial del más allá del sepulcro" (I, 184-85).

Nature kills the individual, but mankind is constantly undergoing a re-creation. Campoamor was deeply impressed by this phenomenon of undying vitality, which convinced him of the superhuman nature of life:

"Muere un hombre y subsiste la familia; perece una genealogía y no se acaba la raza; se extingue la raza y no muere la especie; cuando se anule la especie no se acabará el mundo, y cuando el mundo se acabe subsistirá bajo otra forma el orden del universo" (I, 56).[3]

Inspired by this spectacle, Campoamor could not believe that life was devoid of meaning and doomed to ultimate destruction. Throughout his life, the poet of *el dolor* was an optimist. As he became old, his optimism increased, like that of Browning, and his attacks on pessimists became more frequent and vehement: In *El ideísmo*, he asserts that:

"Job, en medio de su muladar, es bastante más venturoso, creyendo y esperando en la vida futura, que esos pesimistas que acaban por asegurar, de acuerdo con Fichte, 'que este mundo es el peor de los mundos posibles'"[4] (III, 439).

In the last sentence of the book, he proclaims his desire to put an end to:

"Esta verdadera *Danza macabra* moderna, en la cual se baila con pies de huesos todavía con médula, pero ya con caras de risa de calaveras, al son del antiguo tema, reproducido por los pesimistas modernos, que dice: '¡Nada hay peor que la vida! ¡Nada hay mejor que la muerte!' " (III, 546).

---

[3]This is pure Fichte. It is a paraphrase of the famous passage in *Die Bestimmung des Menschen:*
"All death in nature is birth. . . . It is not death that kills, but the more living life, which, concealed behind the old, begins and develops itself. Death and birth are simply the struggle of life with itself, in order that it may manifest itself in every greater glory and greater likeness to itself" (S.W., II, 317f.).

[4]Did Fichte ever make such a remark? It is doubtful, since Fichte was fundamentally an optimist, believing that good would finally triumph over evil in this world. As Xavier Léon says in his book *La philosophie de Fichte* (Paris: Félix Alcan, 1902):
"C'est sur la terre même que la morale de Fichte prétend réaliser le royaume des cieux" (p. 483).
Campoamor was possibly influenced by the legend of Fichte's atheism. *Vide* Robert Adamson, *Fichte* (Edinburgh: William Blackwood, 1881), 57ff.; Wassil Nikoltschoff, *Das Problem des Bösen bei Fichte* (Jena, 1898); Heinrich Rickert, *Fichtes Atheismusstreit* (Berlin, 1899).

However, our enemy of classical philosophy was opposed to the abstract optimism of Malebranche[5] and Leibnitz.[6] This hostility seems to have been inspired by his dislike of the traditional systems. Moreover, although an optimist, he felt that there was little sincerity in these attempts to prove that everything is good, attempts which show a practical indifference to the reality of *el dolor* and which must seem ironical to the mass of suffering mankind (III, 449).

Campoamor's optimism in religious matters would more commonly be called faith. Having declared his distrust in abstract philosophy and its manifestations, and his confidence in the human heart, the ex-traditionalist proceeds, in *El personalismo*, to formulate his belief— completely *a priori*—in a benevolent God:

> "Principio por Dios, por empezar por algo. Pero Dios no es nada, me dirán los racionalistas; no es más que el espectro de vuestra conciencia, el *supongo* de la razón, el personaje de vuestra fantasía. Corriente; yo os dejo con vuestro objeto causa por seguir mi objeto-efecto; yo, que no busco principios, sino fines, que, despreciando el origen de las causas, voy a buscar la ley de los efectos, que no hallando analíticamente ninguna verdad, quiero sólo buscar la síntesis de todas estas mentiras, llamadas naturalezas física y moral, con perdón de los racionalistas, empiezo por esa primera mentira denominada Dios, espectro de mi conciencia, *supongo* de mi razón y personaje de mi fantasía" (I, 34).

This recalls Voltaire's epigram, *"Si Dieu n'existait pas, il faudrait l'inventer,"* which Campoamor later quotes (I, 223). It is likewise similar to the pragmatic religion of James in that the idea of God is based upon its usefulness rather than its objective truth.

> Our optimistic poet proceeds to develop his idea of God:
> "Creo, como mi madre, que Dios es un sér infinitamente bueno, sabio, justo y poderoso. . . ."

Campoamor's divinity embodies all the good and anthropomorphic qualities which Christian theologians attribute to God. One of the great objections of the Spaniard to German philosophy is that the God it creates is impersonal and unsatisfying:

> "En estos sistemas filosóficos *Dios no existe.* Al menos, no es el Dios grande, personal, libre, de atributos infinitos, creado por la

---

[5] *Vide* Henry Joly, *Malebranche* (Paris: Félix Alcan, 1901), chaps. ii and iii.
[6] *Vide* Bertrand Russell, *The Philosophy of Leibniz* (London: George Allen and Unwin, 1900), chap. xv.

intuición universal del género humano, padre de todas los huérfanos, regazo de la esperanza, castigador que nunca ha resistido el arrepentimiento" (I, 323).

In this respect, Campoamor differs not only from German philosophers, but also from Voltaire, whose belief in God sprang from his head rather than from his heart. His attitude resembled rather that of Rousseau, or, even more, of good Spanish Catholics.

(ii) Catholicism

The natural climax to this religious crescendo would seem to be a more or less unqualified adherence to the Catholic faith. However, Campoamor was fundamentally a deist and not a Christian. This point was hotly discussed by the poet's contemporaries, many accusing him of heterodoxy,while his admirers proclaimed the purity of his Catholicism. A careful examination of his writings reveals that he was more than a heterodox; he was not a Catholic, he was not even a Christian.

Occasionally, in his reactionary period, he makes some unctuous reference to Catholicism. When he is speaking his mind, however, his references to the religion of his country are on the whole approving but never filled with conviction. In *El personalismo*, he affirms that:

> "El catolicismo es una especie de tirano atmosférico, del cual es menester respirar algo de su substancia para que la inteligencia sea viable en la región de los cielos" (I, 40).

Campoamor thus implicitly admits his debt to Catholicism as an invaluable influence on his religious development, but nothing more.

Our sceptic put no faith in the fundamental tenets of the Catholic religion. His dislike of Christian dogma was most manifest in his hatred of theology. As he became a reactionary, he wavered in this opposition, but he was never reconciled. In *El ideísmo* (1883), he relates, with malicious humor, how the *cura* of Pilar de la Oradada [sic],[7] "*que ya me está oyendo desde el cielo*," every time the poet returned to Madrid, sent him books of a certain type, the very memory of which gave him a headache. On one occasion, when forwarding the *cura* some money in payment of the books, he took the liberty of writing him the following letter:

---

[7]Campoamor is apparently referring to Pilar de la Horadada, a minute village in the province of Alicante. It is possible that the *cura* became interested in Campoamor while the latter was Governor of Alicante and, perturbed by his unorthodoxy, tried, with the aid of these treatises, to convert him to Catholic dogma.

"Predique usted a nuestros convecinos cosas tan sencillas como éstas, que hay un alma inmortal y un Dios que premia y que castiga y después de puesto Dios en el cielo y la justicia en el alma, no se enfade usted con el sacristán si algún día, dando gusto a nuestros más adorables místicos, amontona hacia el fogón con la escoba de barrer esos libros de moral casuística y dudosa, y muchos de esos mamotretos de teología escolástica de una pesadez y de una inutilidad indudables. Eso en los ejércitos divinos y humanos es lo que se llama la *impedimenta*, que sólo sirve para perder batallas" (III, 448).

Campoamor, therefore, reduces religious dogma to a few tenets which an eighteenth-century deist, such as Voltaire, would approve without any difficulty. Notice that there is no mention of Christ in this passage.

We have already quoted the passage from *Lo absoluto* in which Campoamor pays lip-service to the Catholic cult of Saint Thomas Aquinas. There is a much franker and more significant passage in *El ideísmo*, in which our deist re-affirms his cordial dislike of the theological saint. This antipathy, he confesses, is kept alive in part by a most unpleasant memory. On one occasion, Federico de Madrazo, *"el pintor ideal que, sin detrimento del parecido, hace encantadores hasta los objetos feos,"* was painting portraits of both Jaime Balmes and Campoamor himself.[8] The two met in Madrazo's studio and began a polemic which they later transferred to the press. Campoamor was suffering from a "scholastic indigestion," given him by a priest in Santiago de Compostela who, some years previously, had attempted to teach him Thomistic philosophy. The poet was not very guarded in his language, with the result that Balmes took offense, to the regret and mortification of the deist (III, 462-63).[9]

By opposing theology and attempting to reduce dogma to a minimum, Campoamor destroys the distinguishing features of Christianity and puts it on a level with many other faiths. In *El personalismo* (Book III, chap. ix, "Clave general de la historia"), our deist expounds at length and with a wealth of examples the purely Volterian idea that all religions are fundamentally alike:

---

[8]A reproduction of the portrait of Balmes is to be found in Mariano de Madrazo, *Federico de Madrazo* (in series "Monografías de Arte," Madrid: Saturnino Calleja, 1921), II, lámina 2. The portrait of Campoamor is also well-known, but unfortunately there is no reproduction of it in this work. This is not surprising, since in Madrid alone there were more than four hundred portraits by Federico de Madrazo.

[9]The importance of Saint Thomas Aquinas in Spanish theology and education is brought out by Vicente de la Fuente, "La enseñanza tomística en España," *La Cruz*, March, 1874.

"En el orden moral todos los pueblos del mundo describen a Dios de una misma manera" (I, 103).[10]

The implication is that all religions are equally good. Campoamor's conventional choice of Catholicism is offset by his dislike of many of its features, in particular its Roman tyranny and obscurantism.

Campoamor was consequently devoid of any evangelizing spirit. His Volterian ideas on this subject are frankly expressed in the last Section (VII), entitled "Leyes religiosas," of *Filosofía de las leyes*. It begins thus:

"¿Cual religión es la mejor? La existente, aunque sea falsa. Cuando no exista ninguna religión, estableced la cristiana" (II, 275).[11]

In other words, Christianity is better than nothing.

If Campoamor had no use for Catholic dogma, it was not that he was indifferent to it; he was actively hostile to its most important tenets. Most distasteful to our epicurean was the Catholic conception of Hell, which had been the nightmare of his childhood. There is an interesting autobiographical passage in *El personalismo:*

"He oído hablar tanto [del infierno] que no he oído hablar de otra cosa en mis primeros años. El Dante es un zote, en materia de invenciones de castigos infernales, comparado con algunos de esos malos masculladores de latín que han inventado la máxima: *Haz lo que yo digo y no hagas lo que yo hago*" (I, 257).

The revulsion produced by this experience was lasting, and, even in his reactionary period, Campoamor was nauseated by the idea of Hell. In his *Poética* (1883), he relates how some Catholic friends of his were compiling an album which was to be presented to Pope Leo XIII. They asked our protagonist to contribute some verses. He agreed and wrote in the album a short poem to the effect that, if he were Pope, he would absolve all sinners and close Hell. The more meticulous Catholics were shocked and suggested that Campoamor's leaf be torn out. This proposal was rejected, and the album presented intact to the Pontifex who, on reading the deist's verses, exclaimed benevolently: "Poet, poet!" (III, 376-77).

If Hell does not exist, what is the use of Christ? The essential feature of Christianity is the belief in the divinity of Christ and in His

---

[10]This idea is developed in chap. xii, "Le souper," of Voltaire's *Zadig*.

[11]This idea is to be found in Book XXIV of Montesquieu's *Esprit des Lois*, in particular chap. xxv, "Inconvénient du transport d'une religion d'un pays à un autre," and following chaps. Also Book XXV, chap. xi, "Du changement de religion."

mission to redeem mankind by His most precious blood. Besides rejecting the usual idea of Hell, Campoamor scarcely believed in personal responsibility and considered crime pathological rather than sinful, so that there is no place in his scheme for a Redeemer. His works do not contain any statement suggesting that he really accepted the dogma of Redemption, and it is not difficult to find some which imply that he did not believe in Christ. In the chapter "Religiosidad" of *El personalismo*, Campoamor describes the spirit of adoration characteristic of all religions which consider God as omniscient, omnipotent and ineffably good, he adds:

"Todos los apóstoles que hacen descender a Dios de esta elevación magnífica, en la cual brilla con infinito amor, con infinita sabiduría y con infinita tolerancia, revisten a Dios de sus pasiones y pretenden convertirle como ellos en un detestable faccioso" (I, 223-24).

That Campoamor accepted the then-current theories regarding the non-historicity of Jesus is implied in the following equivocal statement:

"Soy un católico tan invariable que yo jamás renegaré de la *moralidad* del Cristo, por más que las exégetas traten de probarme que no es mentira la *materialidad* del pesebre" (I, 257).[12]

The successors of the crucified Christ were the Martyrs. Like the *philosophes*, Campoamor, in his liberal period, regarded Christian martyrs as insane seekers after glory:

"Casi todo el martirologio cristiano es una prueba evidente de lo agradable que es la muerte para las almas supersticiosas."[13]

Spain is usually considered as a land of saints, but Campoamor had little use for this class in the Christian hierarchy. Indeed, he was irked by the popular devotion enjoyed in Spain by the saints. In his narrative of the journey of Isabel II from Madrid to Alicante and thence by sea to Valencia, he says:

"Son las dos de la mañana y estamos doblando el cabo de San Antonio. Es mucha religiosidad la de los españoles. En Alicante ya hemos

---

[12] *Vide* Weinel and Widgery, *Jesus in the Nineteenth Century and After* (Edinburgh: T. and T. Clark, 1914), chap. ii. It was a disciple of Hegel, David Friedrich Strauss, who first propounded, with solid scholarship, the non-historicity of Christ in his book *Das Leben Jesu, kritisch bearbeitet* (2 vols., 1835-36), which had a great success.

[13] *Filosofía de las leyes*, II, 236-37. Voltaire, in the article "Martyrs" of his *Dictionnaire philosophique* (Paris: Renouard, 1819), affirms that *"On nous berne de martyrs à faire pouffer de rire"* (p. 253). He twits Spaniards with their credulity regarding martyrs (p. 239). Chateaubriand wrote *Les martyrs* (1809) in order to restore the Holy Company of the Martyrs to its former prestige, but Campoamor was evidently not impressed.

visto un castillo de Santa Bárbara, otro de San Fernando, un baluarte de San Carlos, etc., etc., etcétera; ahora estamos doblando un cabo que lo mismo tiene que ver con San Antonio que yo con sus tentaciones, pues maldita la que he tenido hace tiempo, como no sean tentaciones políticas, que suelo tener muchas."[14]

The essential characteristic of a Spanish anticlerical is a strong dislike for *los curas*. He may love and admire Christ, the Martyrs, and the Saints, but the sight of a black cassock must irritate him as the red *muleta* an Iberian *toro de lidia*. According to this acid test, Campoamor is decidedly an anti-clerical.   Once, in conversation, he made the statement:

"Me son profundamente antipáticos las mujeres, los curas, los militares y los príncipes librepensadores."

Anti-clerical Castelar thought fit to circulate this remark made by one posing now as a respectable member of society. Campoamor felt both embarrassed and resentful, but, in his reactionary work *El ideísmo*, he for once shows the courage of his convictions, affirming that *"Lo que dije lo repito"* (III, 420).

For the mass of Catholics, the obvious consequence of the recognition of the existence of sin and Hell, and of the need for redemption, must be repentance. Penitence is an essential part of Christian ethics. However, Campoamor believed that crime, and presumably sin, are produced by ignorance. The remedy is, therefore, not repentance but education:

"Es castigo y la penitencia son dos expiaciones estériles e immorales."[15]

Although he hated the socialism of Rousseau, Campoamor was a direct follower of Jean-Jacques in that he proclaimed the quite un-Christian tenet of the natural goodness of man. *"El hombre es naturalmente bueno,"* he proclaims at the beginning of the chapter "Benevolencia" of *El personalismo* (I, 231).

A common and extreme form of penitence is monasticism. We are not surprised to find that the Christian ideal of cloistered contemplation

---

[14]*Polémicas con la democracia*, II, 655.

[15]*El personalismo*, I, 177. *Vide* Henry Sidgwick, *Outlines of the History of Ethics* (London: MacMillan, 1931), and J. M. Robertson, *A Short History of Morals* (London: Watts, 1920). This scorn of repentance is no philosophical novelty. Spinoza says that "Penitence is not a virtue—that is to say, does not arise from reason; but he who repents of his act is twice miserable or impotent." *Vide* Robertson, 248.

was repugnant to our liberal. In *Filosofía de las leyes*, he devotes a brief but aggressive chapter to "Monasterios":

> "Algunas órdenes religiosas, más bien que instituciones sagradas, parecen sociedades de agiotistas que especulan con uno de los sentimientos más sublimes, la devoción (II, 279).[16]

More personal, more immediate and deeper than his dislike of monasteries was Campoamor's hatred of churches. Like Carducci, he was repelled by their somber lugubriousness. Speaking apparently of some Capuchin church which he frequented in his youth, he relates in *El personalismo*:

> "Cuando me acuerdo de un cierto templo adonde me conducían casi a todas las horas del día, me sucede como cuando alcanzo a ver un cementerio: siento frío. Aquella suciedad tan común en todo lo que no adornan las mujeres, aquella luz semi-extinta, aquel hedor que exhala la carne corrompida, la multitud antijerárquicamente [note] amontonada, calaveras, más profusamente sembradas que las estrellas en el espacio, para representar horriblemente la brevedad de la vida humana; todo este conjunto me hacía entonces recordar la muerte como una especie do *garrote vil*" (I, 258).

The quintessence of Iberian religious sadness is to be found in the typical *Cristos*. Campoamor has expressed in this same autobiographical passage his dislike of these ghostly and ghastly figures:

> "¡Singular manía de terrorizarlo todo! Apuesto a que pocos de mis lectores habrán visto una sola imagen de Cristo que no esté crucificado y archicrucificado. La primera vez que ví un Cristo sin los repugnantes adornos del martirio no le conocía; tan acostumbrado estaba a verlo siempre hecho una lástima" (*loc. cit.*).

In contrast with Campoamor's attitude, the reader inevitably thinks of *El Cristo de Velásquez* of Unamuno.

If churches and their ornaments seemed to Campoamor glacial and inhuman, ecclesiastic ceremonies oppressed him by their monotony and frequency. Speaking of the first sixteen or seventeen years of his life, he says, in the same highly-significant passage from *El personalismo*:

> "Me acuerdo de nuestra religión de *amor* de aquella época como de una horrible *pesadilla*. Por las mañanas me hacían oír todos los días por lo menos una misa. Por el día me enseñaban de una manera

---

[16]Montesquieu has a short chapter (vi) entitled "Des monastères" in his *Esprit des Lois*, Book XXV. It ends thus:

"Ces gens jouent contre le peuple, mais ils tiennent la banque contre lui."

absurda la doctrina cristiana, esa moral divina que, comentada por el fanatismo y la ignorancia, se convierte en un estrecho preceptualismo que hace totalmente imposible la cosa más fácil del mundo: la virtud[!]. Por las noches me hacían rezar el rosario, el cual me acuerdo que yo lo recitaba maquinalmente sin ningún estro interno y sin ritmo exterior. Las multiplicadas prácticas doméstico-religiosas sólo me llenaban de hastío" (I, 257-58).

Even in his reactionary period, Campoamor did not hesitate to proclaim his dislike of church ceremonial. According to a well-known anecdote, Campoamor was once met at the door of a church by León y Castillo, later Spanish Ambassador in Paris,[17] who asked the poet what he was doing. "*Oír misa*," replied the sceptic. "*Cuesta menos trabajo oír misa que oír luego a mi mujer.*"[18]

Campoamor expressed especial dislike for any religious ceremonial or activity smacking of superstition. He has penned in his *Filosofía de las leyes* a chapter entitled "Idolatría" in which he affirms that:

"La monja que besa una reliquia, o el peregrino que anda cien leguas por visitar la Meca, no pasan de ser dos excelentes bobos" (II, 278).

In the same work, Campoamor devotes a brief chapter to condemning the Christian practice of feast-days; with an obvious reference to Spanish Catholicism, he says:

"Más bien que un pueblo de crédulos, parece que alguna religión se ha propuesto crear un pueblo de ociosos" (II, 278).

Such being our philosopher's attitude toward Christianity, it is obvious that he will waste little sympathy on the most Christian period in history: the Middle Ages. In particular, the intellectual inanity of the Middle Ages constituted a theme on which he loved to dwell:

"La filosofía de la Edad media, de esa edad de todas las exageraciones, de todas las andancias, fué exclusivamente *lógica*. Esta es la filosofía de hablar por hablar. Aristóteles y Platón son la Roma y Cartago de estas escuelas de niños grandes."[19]

The legacy of the stupidity of the Middle Ages is, according to Campoamor, clerical education as it was known in the Spain of his time. The teachers at the religious college he attended were monsters of ignorance:

---

[17]Fernando de León y Castillo, Marqués del Muni (1842-1918), who founded *La Revista de España*, was well-known as a liberal and an anti-clerical.

[18]Andrés González Blanco, *Campoamor*, 397.

[19]*El personalismo*, I, 288.

"Cuando yo nací, todavía el clero ejercía una influencia omnímoda sobre la educación. Yo no diré que esto fuese una desgracia, pero al menos para mí no ha sido una dicha. A mi me enseñaron las ciencias físicas mal y las morales peor. Sin que esto sea criticar la instrucción del clero católico [!], diré que los *príncipes de la Iglesia* debían empezar por ser antes los *príncipes de las letras*" (I, 256).

The ignorance of these clerics was exceeded only by their intolerance, and for Campoamor this was the worst of sins. The intolerance of the Catholic Church is another heritage of the Middle Ages:

"He visto tantas veces convertida la religión del amor en un vehículo del odio, los báculos pastorales en garrotes de punta retorcida, las ocasiones de amonestación en actos de censura, los motivos de discusión en motivos de entredicha, las observaciones filosóficas en condenaciones de herejía que, francamente, para el bien de nuestra santa religión yo quisiera que todas las frentes tocadas por el sagrado aceite de las olivas estuviesen antes un poco, ya que no mucho, ungidas por el santo óleo de la inteligencia" (I, 256).

The defects of the Catholic Church, therefore, date back to the Middle Ages, and Campoamor was irritated by its inability to change and to rid itself of its defects. In *El personalismo*, he expresses this idea in an ironical fashion:

"Su petrificación secular, su falta de progresos en la disciplina, que yo antes juzgaba que eran perjudiciales a su existencia, voy creyendo que ayudarán, aunque parásitamente, a hacerle llegar a una edad que no juzgo calculable. . . . Es completamente falso, y esta falsedad es un mérito más" (I, 260-61).

Campoamor became frankly irritated as he perceived the growth of the Neo-Catholic movement, whose adherents, not content with letting the clock stand still, wanted even to turn the hands back. The friction between Campoamor and this group produced a cloud of sparks in the Cortes, where Campoamor was a *diputado*. He made a speech on May 26, 1857, attacking the proposed law of the press, sponsored by Nocedal,[20] which he considered obscurantist. He cried:

---

[20]Cándido Nocedal (1821-1885) became Ministro de la Gobernación in the cabinet which Narváez formed in 1856. He re-established the reactionary constitution of 1845, and acquired even more notoriety by the law of the press against which Campoamor protested. The opposition was in vain; the law was put into effect in July, 1857. Every political newspaper had to be controlled by a responsible editor, who must make a deposit of 1,500 pesetas. Previous censorship was to be exercised. In later years, Nocedal became a member of the Carlist opposition.

"Acabarán por hacer odiosos hasta los Evangelios y santos hasta los murciélagos."

The Neo-Catholic deputy Domingo Moreno protested in a fashion which suggests that, in the above comparison, sparks should be replaced by smoke. He shouted:

"Los evangelios están muy altos."

Campoamor's retort was weak and inexact:
"Es una metáfora."

Nocedal, then Ministro de la Gobernación, and a Neo-Catholic, rose and replied to our still-liberal poet. Campoamor, who was always mortified by the quarrels in which he found himself on account of his imprudent tongue, published a "Rectificación," in which he said, half-repentant and half-resentful:

> "Siento que mi viejo catolicismo haya sido combatido por el neo-catolicismo de los señores Moreno y Nocedal. Si la causa de esta tempestad ha sido el haber pronunciado la palabra *Evangelios*, no tengo inconveniente en cambiarla y sustituírla, ya con mis obras o con disertaciones jurídico-canónicas que puedan escribir los señores Moreno y Nocedal" (II, 301).

This humor seems today flat and childish; indeed, Campoamor's reputation as a wit is largely undeserved, just as was his former reputation as a poet. However, his work is a most valuable document, and that is sufficient for our purpose.

In philosophy, the Neo-Catholic movement represented a return to Saint Thomas Aquinas. We have already discussed Campoamor's attitude toward theology and particularly toward that of Saint Thomas Aquinas. It is not surprising that he should oppose attempts to revive what he considered to be intellectual monstrosities. In *El ideísmo*, Campoamor relates his aforementioned controversy with the high-priest of Spanish Neo-Thomism, Jaime Balmes, who had died meanwhile. Our protagonist, proud of his intellectual ability, dismisses his defunct opponent as *"un pensador muy mediocre"* (III, 462). Even after it had been modified and modernized by Balmes,[21] expressed with attractive

---

[21] Jaime Luciano Balmes (1810-1848), *Obras completas* (Barcelona: Biblioteca Balmes, 1925-27), 33 vols.

Vide Maximiliano Arbodeya Martínez, *Los orígenes de un movimiento social; Balmes, precursor de Ketteler* (Barcelona, Gili, 1912). (For the Christian Socialist movement, discussed later).

sobriety by Padre Ceferino González,[22] and poeticized by *"un orador a quien no le cabe el talento en la cabeza,"* Alejandro Pidal y Mon,[23] Thomistic philosophy still seemed to Campoamor like the magnificent palace of Titus, which all found full of sadness (III, 463-64).

The material manifestation of Neo-Catholicism was the revival of Gothic architecture. Chiefly for economic reasons, the Neo-Gothic movement produced fewer buildings in Spain than in France or in England, but as a theoretical trend it certainly existed, to a much greater degree than might be gathered from its relics. There is a direct contradiction between Campoamor's judgement of Neo-Gothic architecture during his liberal phase and that which he pronounced in his reactionary period. In *El personalismo* (I, 229), he affirms cynically that every creed is composed of a thousandth part of conviction and of nine hundred and ninety-nine of illusion; that Catholics thus imagine that prayers uttered under an ogival arch are more acceptable to God than those said in the Mosque of Córdoba, converted into a Christian temple, or in St. Paul's in London which, being of Græco-Roman architecture, seems to arouse pagan ideas. In *El ideísmo* (III, 492-94), on the contrary, he accuses the Renascence, and more especially Michael Angelo, of destroying the truly Christian art of the Middle Ages. He

---

Buenaventura de Córdoba, *Noticia histórico-literaria del Dr. D. Jaime Balmes* (Madrid, Eusebio Aguado, 1848).

Benito García de los Santos, *Vida de Balmes* (Madrid: Sociedad de Operarios, 1848).

José Elías de Molins, *Balmes y su tiempo* (Barcelona: Imprenta Barcelonesa, 1906).

Narciso Roure y Figueras, *Actualidad y excelencia del pensamiento de Balmes* (Madrid: La España Moderna, 1911).

Narciso Roure y Figueras, *La Vida y las obras de Balmes* (Madrid: Perlado Páez, 1910).

Eustaquio Ugarte de Ercilla, S. J., *Acerca de la filosofía de Balmes* (Madrid: Razón y Fe, 1922).

Eustaquio Ugarte de Ercilla, S. J., *Balmes* (Madrid: Razón y Fe, 1921-23).

A. Lugan, *Balmès* (Paris: Tralin, 1911).

[22]Ceferino González y Díaz Tuñón (1831-1894) was one of the best-known prelates of nineteenth-century Spain. In 1864, he published his *Estudios sobre la filosofía de Santo Tomás*. In 1883, he became Archbishop of Seville and was made cardinal the following year. In 1885, he rose to the primacy of Toledo but could not stand the climate and returned to Seville the next year. His *Historia de la filosofía* was republished several times. At his funeral, the Government paid him the highest tribute.

[23]Alejandro Pidal y Mon (1846-1913) studied Thomistic philosophy under Fray Ceferino González. Pidal y Mon's father was Spanish Ambassador to the Holy See. Of Don Alejandro's fifteen children, three girls became nuns. Pope Leo XIII granted him the Grand Cross of the Order of Saint Gregory the Great. Campoamor is referring in particular to his book *Santo Tomás de Aquino, su vida, historia de sus obras, su doctrina* (1875).

relates that, when he was in London, he could not understand why the Houses of Parliament were not St. Paul's Cathedral, and St. Paul's Cathedral was not the Houses of Parliament. These two references to London suggest, although Campoamor does not say so, that he was more or less consciously revising his judgment. Quite logical from the Neo-Gothic standpoint, but decidedly startling in a traditionalist, is Campoamor's attack on the Escorial, which he puts in the same class as Saint Paul's:

"El Escorial . . . . más que al Dios grande, debía estar dedicado al gran marido de Juno. El Escorial, comido por las sierras del Guadarrama, es, entre estas, una colina más, y supongo que habrá sido un capricho de Felipe II, impuesto a Juan de Herrera, lo de adornar el templo exteriormente con aquellas torrecitas laterales que dicen que imitan en su conjunto al asador en que fué martirizado San Lorenzo y que, como el utensilio está al revés, ni siquiera le ha podido inspirar al diablo el modelo para hacer unas parrillas que le sirviesen en el infierno para tostar herejes."[24]

The reader should be informed that this is a witticism. This curious passage begins as an attack on the un-Christian, neo-classical architecture of the Escorial, but it develops into a malicious satire of the monastery-mausoleum embodying the Catholic spirit of martyrdom and the Spanish cult of those infernal torments which had been the nightmare of Campoamor's youth. It is interesting to see how thin was the renegade's conservative crust and how easily the latent liberal could bubble up through the cracks.

Neo-Catholicism represented one attempt to revitalize a decadent institution. A similar and, as we have seen in studying Pardo-Bazán, probably more successful effort was made by the Christian Socialist movement. Campoamor was as hostile to it as he was to Neo-Catholicism, and thus found himself in another argument with Castelar. This notorious anti-clerical leaned toward Christian Socialism and, in his *Fórmula del progreso* (1857), asserted that *"El cristianismo es el ideal religioso de la democracia."* Scorning ambages, Campoamor justifiably retorted that this remark *"es una de la muchas frases sin sentido de que usa el señor Castelar."*[25] He rightly affirms that the natural consequence of democracy is the freedom of cults and diversity of religion.

---

[24]Concerning these well-known details, *vide* D. Zurbitu, S. I., *San Lorenzo de El Escorial* (Madrid: Razón y Fe, 1929), and Albert F. Calvert, *The Escorial* (London: John Lane, the Bodley Head, 1907).

[25]*Polémicas con la democracia*, II, 412. This was merely an incident in the heated controversy provoked by the *Fórmula del progreso*. *La Democracia*, a newspaper founded

Our analysis of Campoamor's attitude toward Christianity shows quite clearly that, although, throughout his life, he remained a professing member of the orthodox Catholic Church, he was, in his most fertile years, fundamentally a non-Christian, indeed an anti-Christian, and that, even in his reactionary period, his Catholicism was very flimsy. It is not surprising, then, that the more orthodox Catholics regarded him with suspicion. In particular, Padre Ceferino González, Archbishop of Seville, in his *Historia de la filosofía*[26] indicted the poet on the count of orthodoxy, and, like Valera, accused him of pantheism. Even in *El ideísmo*, Campoamor replies jocosely:

"Pobre Dios Pan, tan inofensivo como un cocinero y tan dormilón como un borracho alcoholizado!" (III, 464).

What is surprising is that few or none seem to have realized how grave and utter was the poet's heresy.

(iii) The Religion of Campoamor

What then was the religion of Campoamor? Its fundamental tenet was negative: an insistence upon tolerance, which our deist considered to be the hallmark of civilization. Holding that all sincere religions are equally good, Campoamor preferred Christianity only for social convenience and was deeply opposed to the forceful imposition of any faith. In *El personalismo*, he uses two metaphors to express his conviction:

"La tolerancia es el barómetro de la civilización; todo pueblo, cuanto más salvaje es, es más intolerante. . . . El fanatismo es un burro que bebe sangre" (I, 224).[27]

In order to prove his contention that "*Todos los grandes hombres hacen de la intolerancia el blanco de sus más acerbas invectivas*," Campoamor proceeds to give a series of quotations from Plato, Diogenes, La Harpe, Clement XIV, Origen, Pythagoras, Guizot, Marmontel, Frederick the Great, Voltaire and Mahomet. Even in his reactionary period, Campoamor constantly proclaimed his deep attachment to tolerance: a curiously un-Spanish attitude. In *El ideísmo*, he explains that the natural fruit of his beloved *metafísica* is tolerance:

by Castelar, and *La Discusión*, also a liberal paper, engaged in a broadside battle. Carlos Rubio y Collet (1832-1871) also attacked the *Fórmula* from the columns of *La Iberia*. *Vide infra*.

[26]2nd edit., Madrid, 1886.

[27]"Qu'est-ce que la tolérance? c'est l'apanage de l'humanité."—Voltaire, *Dictionnaire philosophique*, art. "Tolérance."

"Una buena clasificación de los principios metafísicos podría producir el inapreciable bien de difundir la más social de las virtudes, que es la tolerancia. Según el principio metafísico de que se parta, todo el mundo puede tener razón. Para el que parte de una base metafísica *ontológica*, el más sabio es el que tiene más fe; el mayor filósofo, Santo Tomás, y el mejor poeta Calderón. Para el que toma la substancia *cósmica* como principio de las cosas, el más sabio es el más materialista; el más filósofo, Espinosa, y el más sublime artista, Anacreonte. Para los psicólogos que creen que el *yo* es la medida de todo, Protágoras es el más sabio; Fichte, el más gran filósofo y Leopardi, el mayor artista" (III, 429).

This nebulous and almost meaningless passage reveals what an obsession *la metafísica* constituted for Campoamor in his reactionary years. Yet it is a satisfaction to see that the poet's youthful attachment to tolerance was a well-fed flame which even reaction could not stifle.

The basis of Campoamor's religious belief was materialistic determinism, which, out of respect for established religion, he labelled "Providence." In *El personalismo* (I, 154), he points out that if the human mind had enough energy and power of synthesis, it could trace the dust constituting the tile with which an old hag killed Pyrrhus back to breezes in the Garden of Eden. In his attempts to harmonize theology and science, Campoamor enunciates something approaching pantheism:

"Las leyes naturales son preceptos divinos."

It is not clear whether he admits the possibility of miracles, but everything suggests that he does not. This materialistic determinism does not include the human world, but it surrounds it so closely as to leave it little freedom.

He proceeds to use natural determinism as a basis for predestination: "La predestinación humana es una ley natural" (I, 156).

However, he does not give to predestination its traditional meaning of the inevitability of every action great or small. For Campoamor, predestination means the small circle to which the activities of each individual are restricted.

Within these limits, a man can become master of one speciality: "En su esfera de acción todo hombre ha nacido para ser un genio, para ser un César. La Sabiduría divina no ha criado más que especialidades" (I, 156).

Thus Campoamor would seem to reject as impossible the Renascence ideal of the complete man. His theory of specialities clashes even with the eighteenth-century ideology on which he had been nourished: which commended encyclopedism and praised *l'honnête homme*. This belief in specialization sounds singularly modern.

Within this narrow circle, man has an amount of free-will proportionate to his degree of development. As he increases in intelligence, so man rises above the animal world and enjoys more true freedom. More rights should be given to him, and more responsibility demanded of him:

> "La *responsabilidad* personal está en razón directa del *grado* de personalidad. A más personalidad, más *derechos* y más *deberes*. A menos inteligencia, menos *deberes* y menos *derechos*" (I, 169).

Campoamor reproaches theologians and jurists for having supposed that men possess free-will, and for having made far too heavy demands upon them. Campoamor shows that he was in advance of his time by demanding that delinquents be treated, not as wilful criminals, but as organic misfits.

Campoamor's conception of Hell is typical of the philosophy of the Romantic period. Like George Sand, he protested vigorously against the Catholic idea of Hell. According to him, punishment in the afterworld consists of remorse, an idea similar to that expressed by Victor Hugo in "Caïn":

> "Allí pasan y repasan por ante nuestra inteligencia todos nuestros actos detestables, todas nuestras palabras deshonestas, todos nuestros pensamientos indignos, y torturan el sentimiento en una crucifixión moral más íntima y más inexorable que el dolor que excitaría en un hombre solo el acumulamiento de los dolores de todos los heridos por la fiereza, de los males de todas las víctimas de la procacidad y las vergüenzas de todos los los zaheridos por la maledicencia. Este es el *infierno*" (I, 252).

Such is Campoamor's Hell. But what about his Heaven? Of this he has given us no corresponding picture: indeed, he makes practically no reference to it. Life in a supernatural world was obviously a concept beyond his spiritual bounds. Like Voltaire, he believed in a God who rewarded in Heaven those who had lived well on Earth, but to him, as to Voltaire, this knowledge meant very little.

CHAPTER IV

PHILOSOPHY OF ART

THE most complete exposition of Campoamor's ideas concerning art is to be found in his *Poética*. This work was based on a paper which he read in the Madrid Ateneo on the night of March 29, 1879, as an inaugural address for the prose-readings which the Ateneo had established (III, 213). To this he added some of his other papers on the same subject. The first edition appeared at Madrid in 1883, the second, containing many additions, at Valencia in 1890. Since Campoamor's literary ideas have only an indirect bearing on our subject, they are not discussed in great detail here.

The basis of Campoamor's artistic philosophy was a strong dislike of academic poetry, on which his mind had been nourished during his early years. Although he hated artificial verse-productions, he succeeded in mastering the technique so well that his *liceo* took the exceptional course of publishing his first verses, while his preceptor, a certain Señor Zaragoza, assured him that he was like Boabdil in Granada, that is to say the *Rey Chico* of Spanish poetry.[1] However, Campoamor soon recovered from this misdirected training and came to realize how sterile his efforts had been. In his dislike of academic poetry, he showed his affiliations with the romantic movement and, for once, detached himself from eighteenth-century France.

He rejoins the tradition of the *philosophes* when he affirms that poetry must deal with the problems of the epoch:

"La poesía verdaderamente lírica debe reflejar los sentimientos personales del autor en relación con los problemas propios de su época."[2]

Yet, even in this definition, Campoamor dissociates himself from the *philosophes* in that he stresses the sentiments of the poet. By sentiment, he understands the intimacy of say Bécquer, and certainly not the expansiveness of Zorrilla. In *El personalismo*, he explains ironically that since, as Spinoza says, God, the infinite substance, is divided into thought and extension, he recognized, as soon as he began writing poetry, that there was nothing for him to do but to take refuge in the realm of thought, for Zorrilla filled every inch of the attribute of extension:

---

[1] *El personalismo*, I, 278.
[2] Quoted by Andrés González-Blanco, *Campoamor*, 151.

"Viendo la totalidad de la naturaleza externa abarcada por la mente objetiva de este bardo divino, no tuve más remedio que refugiarme en el campo de mis impresiones subjetivas, íntimas, completamente personales" (I, 279).

It is easy to be even more precise concerning Campoamor's use of the word sentiment. He entertains a rather melancholy outlook on life in that for him sentiment means above all sorrow—*el dolor*. He holds that sorrow is the essence of human feeling:

"En este subterráneo de la vida, por donde caminamos agobiados bajo la bóveda del pesar, hasta que salgamos a la luz, hasta que nos despojemos de nuestra carga mortal, el dolor es nuestro compañero más aborrecido, más consecuente y más íntimo. ¡El dolor! Voz del cielo, divino mensajero que nos anuncia la futura redención de nuestro espíritu, ay que lanza un ser infinito, completamente subjetivo, completamente personal, al separarse de su compañera la materia" (I, 100).

This is a romantic, almost a mystic, interpretation of *el dolor*. It is curious to note that in the same work, *El personalismo*, Campoamor later gives a totally different explanation of sorrow, one more in accord with the epicurean philosophy of the eighteenth century and incidentally with modern psychology. He says that, if men are unhappy, it is because they are not content to accept the limitations which Fate has placed upon them:

"Dios nos ha criado para ser felices. ¿En qué consiste, pues, que la mayor parte de los hombres somos desgraciados? En que nos revelamos [rebelamos] contra nuestro destino, saliéndonos de nuestra esfera de actividad moral" (I, 157).

This is what a psychologist would call "maladjustment." Even in this passage, it is necessary to note the allusion to God, and the half-romantic, half-Franciscan reference to destiny.

It was from the word *dolor* that Campoamor coined his famous neologism, *dolora*, which provoked such heated discussions. Juan Nicasio Gallego thought the word too new and replaceable by the Portuguese word *magoa*.[3] The Marqués de Pidal[4] was strongly opposed to any

---

[3] *Magoa* (or *magua*), from *macula*, literally a stain, a bruise, or a blow, is thus defined in its figurative meaning by Domingos Vieira, in his *Thesouro da lingua portugueza* (Oporto: Ernesto Chadron, 1873): "Dôr d'alma, affliccão, pezar, amargura." Juan Nicasio Gallego (born 1777) was an old man at the time and very conservative. He died in 1853, so that his opposition to the word *dolora* disappeared at that date.

such substitution. When Campoamor entered the Spanish Academy, his *padrino*, the Marqués de Molins,[5] referred to the now-popular word as a *"neologismo audazmente propagado,"* and, in his reply to the poet's *discurso de entrada*, pronounced this prophesy:

"Los poetas la conocen, los aficionados la cultivan, los curiosos la aplauden, las damas la sienten y la Academia, no lo dudéis, admitiendo al autor, la dará carta de naturaleza."[6]

Over half a century passed, and the Academy showed no desire to admit the word to its Dictionary. This could at first be explained by the deep dislike which the then Director of the Academy, Francisco Martínez de la Rosa, entertained for Campoamor.[7] In later years, however, the inaction could only be attributed to the corporation's notorious inertia. The neologism was finally admitted in the 1925 edition of the *Diccionario*, where it is thus defined:

"DOLORA (Nombre inventado por el poeta Campoamor, hacia 1846) f. Breve composición poética de espíritu dramático, que envuelve un pensamiento filosófico sugerido generalmente por los contrastes de la vida o las ironías del destino, etc."

Las doloras, both the word and the work, drew Campoamor into a public controversy which he always recalled with great bitterness. His enemies referred to him, with scornful antonomasia, as *"el autor de las Doloras."* To his defense rushed several minor critics who thus won Campoamor's lasting gratitude[8]: Carolina Coronado de Perry,[9] Navarrete,[10] Hurtado,[11] and the Marqués de Auñón.[12]

---

[4]Undoubtedly Pedro José Pidal (1800-1865), first Marqués de Pidal and father of Alejandro Pidal y Mon.

[5]Mariano Roca de Torgores y Carrasco (1812-1889) was made first Marqués de Molins by Isabel II in 1848. He organized in the Palacio de Villahermosa literary *veladas*, in which Campoamor acquired fame as a poet. During the years following 1868, he was the *decano* of the *grandeza de España*; as such, he wrote the letter of adhesion which the Spanish grandees sent to the Prince of Asturias, later Alfonso XII.

[6]*Discursos leídos en las recepciones públicas que ha celebrado desde 1847 la Real Academia Española* (Madrid: Imprenta Nacional, 1865), III, 200.

[7]Martínez de la Rosa died in 1862, and was succeeded by the Duque de Rivas. Upon Angel Saavedra's decease three years later (1865), he was followed by Campoamor's protector, the Marqués de Molins, who was Director until 1889. It is astounding that he did not facilitate the acceptance of the word *dolora*.

[8]*El personalismo*, I, 380.

[9]*Vide* Juan Valera, *Obras completas*, XXXIII, 240-47.

[10]Ramón Navarrete y Fernández Landa (1818-1897), journalist and playwright.

[11]Antonio Hurtado y Valhondo (1825-1878), a once-famous poet and playwright.

[12]This Marqués de Auñón is forgotten except for the introduction he wrote to Victoriano Pérez y García's book, *Pensamientos y máximas filosófico-católicas de los*

Our poet later became involved in a more significant polemic. The genesis of it is related in chapter xii, entitled "¿La forma poética está llamada a desaparecer?" of *La poética*; it constitutes an addition to the second edition, that of Valencia (1890). Three sections of the Ateneo, those of *Ciencias morales y políticas, Ciencias físicas y naturales*, and *Ciencias históricas*, decided to publish in conjunction a review entitled *El Ateneo*, under the joint editorship of their three presidents. A prospectus was issued in which it was said that "*se insertará toda producción referente a cualquier rama de la ciencia, sin desdeñar la poesía.*" The reference to poetry was really a gracious homage, since the sections which were founding the review did not include literature. Admittedly the title *Ateneo* was general and rather presumptuous. Campoamor, in an article published in *La Ilustración Española y Americana*,[13] expressed deep irritation at what he considered a patronizing attitude toward poetry. He fired a salvo of insults at the offending members and asked if the Ateneo wished to revive the famous discussion as to whether the poetic form was destined to disappear (III, 336). This was apparently a rhetorical question, for Campoamor, without waiting for an answer, launched into a long defense of poetry, which, he asserts, will never, never die. He was referring to an earlier skirmish in the Ateneo mentioned in *La metafísica y la poesía* (III, 393-94). The positivist Juan Valera had organized a symposium of members of the Ateneo, who discussed poetry from the scientific or rather utilitarian standpoint and reached the conclusion that it was destined to disappear. It was no doubt for this reason that the editor of *El Ateneo*, finding himself under fire from Campoamor, asked Valera to take up his defense. Valera acceded, and it was in this way that the polemic concerning *La metafísica y la poesía* began.[14] We have already mentioned it in discussing Campoamor's metaphysics. It was devoted largely to *la metafísica*, but a considerable amount of space was given to the original action in the realm of poesy. Campoamor displayed as much energy in this fight as in the main affray.

---

immortales genios y profundos pensadores D. J. Balmes, P. Raulica, P. Felix, Marqués de Valdegamas, Vizconde de Bonald, Conde de Maistre, etc.

[13] *Vide* Juan Valera, *Obras completas*, XXXVI, 177. This volume contains the articles of both Valera and Campoamor concerning *La metafísica y la poesía*. It appeared in 1913 and reproduced the original edition published by Sáenz de Jubera Hermanos in 1891 (*vide supra*). It is preceded by *Metafísica a la ligera* (pp. 11-138), a collection of articles by Valera devoted to Campoamor's book *El ideísmo*. Valera tells us (p. 141) that *El Ateneo* was already dead; its life must have been very short. It was revived for a few years in January, 1906, appearing each month thereafter until July, 1912.

[14] *Vide* Juan Valera, *Obras completas*, XXXVI, 141.

However, at times, during his reactionary period, Campoamor showed indifference toward poetry, not for positivistic, but on the contrary for idealistic, reasons. He tended to regard art as a frivolous occupation in comparison with the serious problems of fate and eternity: He asks, in *Lo absoluto:*

"¿No es verdad que las más sublimes manifestaciones de las artes . . . . parecen puerilidades agradables, buenas sólo para entretener la voluptuosidad de las mujeres de ingenio, pero indignas de pre-ocupar ni por un momento la razón varonil de ningún hombre de estudio?" (I, 676).

In condemning everything not related to eternity as frivolous and futile, Campoamor rejoins the Castilian ascetic tradition

CHAPTER V

SOCIOLOGICAL IDEAS

THE social ideas of Campoamor are summarized in the simple words of the title of one of Salvador de Madariaga's books: *Jerarquía o anarquía*. For Campoamor, society is impossible without a hierarchy, and those attempting to simplify the complexity of the social hierarchy are really destroying society. In a characteristic tirade in *El personalismo*, he enumerates those engaged in this nihilistic task: priests acting in the name of humanity, kings in the name of unity, democrats in the name of equality, politicians in the name of society, and philosophers in the name of the "absolute" human spirit. He concludes with a typical insult:

"¡Asesinos! y más que asesinos ¡necios!" (I, 90-91).

This might seem to be an ultra-conservative attitude, although Campoamor first propounded these ideas in his liberal youth. Rather is this an expression of the Spaniard's Volterianism. Campoamor's hierarchy, in theory at least, is not based on tradition, but solely on intellectual ability. As he explains in *El personalismo:*

"Los grados de la inteligencia siempre marcarán los grados de la responsabilidad social, moral o religiosa, siempre serán el termómetro de la *personalidad*. La inteligencia puede ser más o menos *cuantitativa*, pero siempre es igualmente *cualitativa*. El hombre es tanto más hombre cuánto más piensa. Y el hombre es tanto menos hombre cuanto menos piensa" (I, 92-93).

Campoamor's psychology would seem to be primitive in that it is derived from the ultra-Herbartian idea that intelligence can be measured as it were with a foot-rule. This fallacy is based on the misconception that intelligence is all of one quality, and differs only in quantity. Campoamor had of course never heard of Spearman and the G-theory. He would seem, moreover, to be a dangerous theorizer in that he wished to correlate the personality (i.e. intelligence) of every individual member of society with his public rights and duties, completely disregarding the intrinsic inertia of society.

Being an aristocrat of the intellect, Campoamor had no use for any idealization of the Spanish people, *el pueblo*, especially in its more colorful aspects. This form of patriotism, or, as Campoamor would say, *patrioterismo*, was assiduously cultivated by writers such as Castelar. Insinuating that Campoamor was a snob who tried to hide his humble origin, Castelar said pointedly:

"Yo no olvido que he nacido en cuna plebeya."[1]

Campoamor retorted that he was disgusted with Castelar's glorification of the vulgar elements in the Spanish tradition:

"Es inútil, completamente inútil, que el señor Castelar me obra su tienda de quincalla patriotera, donde muestra a los demócratas lugareños sus puñales de hoja de lata a lo Bruto y sus braseros pintados a lo Scévola; yo he llegado ya a ese fin de la juventud, que es la aurora de los desengaños, y, cuando veo un puesto de esas baratijas, exclamo como Socrates: "¡Cuántas cosas que a nadie sirven para nada!" (II, 446).

Admittedly, Campoamor wrote these lines during his reactionary period.

Our aristocrat of the intellect was then a bitter opponent of any form of social levelling and a fanatical apostle of the idea of hierarchy. In the application of this principle, Campoamor followed closely the theories of Saint-Simon. Every individual, he says, must be rewarded according to the post he fills, and posts must be allotted according to merit. Weary, no doubt, of the recurrence of an expression he hated, *Liberté, Egalité, Fraternité*, he affirmed that the best possible state would be that in which every public building bore the inscription:

"A cada uno según su capacidad y a cada capacidad según su mérito."[2]

This remark, which is not easy to analyze, is a translation of Saint-Simon's aphorism:

"A chacun selon sa capacité, à chaque capacité selon ses œuvres."[3]
The meaning of this sentence is made more confused by the use of *mérito* instead of *œuvres*.

A social hierarchy reflected in the distribution of wealth is naturally incompatible with the communization of property, which, despite his affiliations with the French humanitarians, Campoamor always repulsed. His realistic sense is evident in this affirmation:

"Todos los socialistas modernos que han fundado sus sistemas sobre la base de la propiedad común han partido de un imposible, porque dos instintos fundamentales, el yo y el deseo de adquirir, rechazan la propiedad colectiva y tienden naturalmente a apropiarse las cosas con exclusión de cualquier otro partícipe" (I, 194).

---

[1] *Vide Polémicas con la democracia* II, 438.

[2] *El personalismo*, I, 117.

[3] *Vide Doctrine de Saint-Simon. Exposition. Première année*, ed. C. Bouglé et Elie Halévy (Paris: Marcel Rivière, 1924).

It was the question of personal property which separated Campoamor
from Rousseau; he quotes with approval Voltaire's satires of his rival's
communistic ideas. Jean Jacques was dead and gone before, but his
spirit still lived in Pierre-Joseph Proudhon, whose famous dictum, in
his first *Mémoire sur la propriété* (1840), was undoubtedly ringing in
Campoamor's ears:

> "La propriété, c'est le fait le plus injuste qui soit au monde, c'est
> le vol!"[4]

Campoamor feared communism also because it meant a loss of liberty.
He was a liberal in the literal sense of demanding all possible liberty
within the limits of reasonableness: He cries, in *El personalismo:*

> "Desportillad, desportillad todas las esclusas que se oponen a la
> expasión de todas las libertades lícitas; no nos condenéis a la esterili-
> dad por temor a un exceso de fecundación. ¡Vengan las inundaciones
> morales!" (I, 119).

The final exclamation is closely paralleled by Unamuno's:

> "Fe, fe en la espontaneidad propia, fe en que siempre seremos noso-
> tros, y venga la inundación se fuera, la ducha."[5]

Metaphors involving a moral shower-bath were common among Spanish
social writers of the last century.

Campoamor was truly Iberian in his dislike of social institutions
which cramp the *Yo*. In an ecstatic passage of *El personalismo*, he
repudiates all those fetters which have been invented to bind down the
individual:

> "El *género humano*, el *Estado*, la *sociedad*, la *patria*, personajes
> impersonales, espíritus ficticios de cuerpos verdaderos, fundiciones
> revertidoras de la personalidad al caos no son más que la explotación
> del hombre por la nada . . . . en las academias se funde el individuo
> para verterlo líquido en la especie, en los palacios se anula el súbdito
> para dar realidad al déspota, en los comicios se suicida el ciudadano
> para dar vida a esa mistificación tenebrosa, a ese fantasma volun-
> tarioso y feroz, indeterminado e indeterminable, denominado patria"
> (I, 351).

As we shall see, it was his love of liberty and hatred of totalitarianism
which separated the Spaniard from German political thought.

---

[4] *Vide* Gaston Isambert, *Les idées socialistes en France de 1815 á 1848* (Paris: Félix
Alcan, 1905), chap. ix.

[5] *Ensayos*, I, 214.

The only natural institution, says Campoamor, is the family, and man's only natural obligation is toward the family. Apart from this restriction, he must assert his personality. Harking back to the eighteenth-century eulogies of the *père de famille*, Campoamor cries:

"¡Padres de familia! Vamos a establecer un *feudalismo personal*; . . . ¡padres de familia! ¡A ser semi-reyes! . . . a ser casi-pontífices" (I, 352).

Our happy husband was doubtless influenced in this matter by the Victor Hugo of "Lorsque l'enfant paraît."

Campoamor does not establish his "personal feudalism" in order that individuals may behave like robber-barons. Rather does he hope that, enhanced with this new dignity, man will make himself worthy of his position:

"Antes de adorar a nadie, empecemos por aconsejar al hombre que se haga digno de adorarse a sí mismo" (I, 352).

Joining the movement which found its most eloquent expression in Victor Hugo's *Dernier jour d'un condamné* (1829) and *Les misérables* (1862), Campoamor attacked the traditional view of crime as a natural expression of personality let loose, and devoted several chapters of *El personalismo* to proving that crime is pathological, a disease in man's otherwise noble nature. Punishment, instead of cure, and above all capital punishment, he condemns as barbarous. He compares the death sentence to the act of an angry, stupid, and spoiled child, who smashes a toy which does not work because he lacks the skill and patience necessary to put its mechanism right. Where Society sees crime, the law-maker should perceive sickness (I, 179). Society fails to make adequate provision for the moral and intellectual education of people, and then punishes them because they have not learned.[6]

In order to facilitate this problem, and to avoid burdening society with children it could not adequately educate, Campoamor, at least in his liberal period, was a convinced partisan of birth-control. He affirms, in his *Filosofía de las leyes*, that the strength of a state lies rather in quality than quantity. Governments should forbid the marriage of those having any inherent physical or mental defect. Campoamor is not hostile even to the idea of Stewart,[7] that governments should prohibit

---

[6]Campoamor was following Beccaria, Bentham, Feuerbach, etc. *Vide* Raymond Saleilles, *The Individualization of Punishment* (Boston: Little, Brown, 1911), chap. iii.

[7]Campoamor is undoubtedly referring to Dugald Stewart, who discusses the matter in his essay "Of Population," *Collected Works of Dugald Stewart* (Edinburgh: Thomas Constable, 1855), VIII, 59ff. However, Stewart does not make, at least there, the proposal Campoamor attributes to him.

the marriage of those who are too poor to support children.   The Spanish
liberal was a Malthusian in that he believed that the population was
increasing more rapidly than the means of subsistence, and he urged
the government to take the necessary steps in order to keep the relationship stable.   He distinguishes two means of controlling the birth-rate.
The first is instruction, and by this he apparently means dissemination
of the ideas advocated by Malthus.   The second is the establishment of
bordellos:

> "Con las mancebías se impiden muchos matrimonios inconsiderados,
> haciendo que el hombre satisfaga, sin deplorables consecuencias, una
> de sus inclinaciones más incontinentes y más intensas" (II, 247).

Campoamor proceeds to demand government inspection of brothels in
order to prevent venereal disease.[8]   This radical attitude toward sex
problems in the Catholic Spain of nearly a century ago is surprising.   It
was justifiable, in that the birth-rate was extremely high, although,
through inadequate care, a large percentage of the babies died.[9]   Likewise, in his liberal period, Campoamor regarded marriage as a natural
institution and thus, by implication, deprived it of its divine nature:

> "No quiero dejar de repetir que la asociación matrimonial [note the
> expression] es un estado natural, y es natural porque es feliz, y es
> feliz porque en él se satisfacen todas nuestras propensiones afectivas.
> . . . La sensualidad, el amor a la prole, la amistad, el deseo de ad-
> quirir, la inclinación a lo bello, el instinto de mando, etcétera, son
> sentimientos que, clamando colectivamente por satisfacción, arras-
> tran a los hombres al estado del matrimonio como a un centro donde
> confluyen todos nuestros caprichos y deseos" (II, 259).

Despite this "philosophical" concept of marriage, Campoamor approves
of the canonical prohibition of divorce, since he believes that a stable
family is a social necessity.

The Moorish, androcratic strain in Campoamor is revealed in his
hostility, even during his liberal period, toward those advocating equality
of the sexes.   He held that women are naturally inferior, and, apparently,
that it was they who would have to make any necessary sacrifices in

---

[8]For a historical bibliography of all these delicate questions, *vide* the massive *Biblio-
graphie des ouvrages relatifs à l'amour, aux femmes, au mariage*, 4th ed., by J. Lemonnyer;
Paris, 1894-1900, 4 vols.

[9]*Vide* José Gómez Ocaña, *El sexo, el hominismo y la natalidad* (Madrid: Saturnino
Calleja, 1919), Part III; M. T. Nisot, *La question eugénique dans les divers pays* ("Publi-
cations de l'Association Internationale pour la Protection de l'Enfance"; Bruxelles, 1929),
II, 276-280.

order to avoid disintegration of the family. In the same liberal work, the *Filosofía de las leyes*, he asserts that:

"Algunos escritores, más galantes que cuerdos, han querido proclamar la emancipación del sexo hermoso. . . . La mayoría de las mujeres tienen una organización más imperfecta que la mayoría de los hombres, y por eso serán eternamente esclavas, porque les leyes naturales se obedecen irremisiblemente, y es una ley natural que los más débiles obedezcan a los más fuertes" (II, 261-62).

Notice that the relationship of the sexes is based, not on any divine precept, but upon a natural law.[10]

In a paradoxical way, Campoamor displayed a more liberal attitude toward women during his reactionary period. The reason was simply that the pessimists, whom our protagonist attacked so vehemently in his later years, had undertaken, as a reaction against romantic feminism, a campaign to disparage women. In *El ideísmo*, Campormor refers to "*las impotencias acaso no sólo intelectuales de Schopenhauer[11] y Leopardi,*"[12] and describes this campaign as "stupid." He blames the positivists for beginning the trouble, but he has to confess that Comte himself was not responsible, since the adoration of woman formed an important part in his religion of humanity, both a public and a private cult being recommended (III, 420).[13] It is probable that Campoamor's happy married life contributed to weaken the anti-feminism of his impetuous youth.

---

[10]Compare Montesquieu, *L'esprit des lois*, Book XVI, chap. ii, "Que dans les pays du midi il y a dans les deux sexes une inégalité naturelle."

[11]Admittedly, Schopenhauer regards love as an illusion. *Vide* Richard Hohenemser, *Arthur Schopenhauer als Psychologe* (Leipzig: Johann Ambrosius Barth, 1924), 227-238.

[12]It is unjust to describe Leopardi as anti-feminist. He suffered from erotic enthusiasm and condemned women only in moments of disgust. *Vide* N. Serban, *Léopardi sentimental* (Paris: Edouard Champion, 1913), Livre I; Luigi Tonnelli, *Leopardi* (Milan: Corbaccio, 1937), chap. vii.

[13]*Vide* Ernest Seillière, *Auguste Comte* (Paris: Félix Alcan, 1924), III, chap. ii, "La religion de la femme."

CHAPTER VI

IDEAS CONCERNING GOVERNMENT

DESPITE his affiliations with poetry, Campoamor displayed, in discussing problems, an astonishing thisworldliness. It is most evident in his concept of the state, which is completely devoid of mysticism. He disliked the impractical character of Rousseau's theories, in particular his communism, but he seems to have imbued the idea of *le contrat social*. As he says in the picturesque language of *El personalismo:*

"El estado es una caja de cambio, donde se impone en deber y se recoge un derecho equivalente. Unos imponen su hacienda, otros, su sangre, otros su inteligencia, y todos reciben a trueque poder, honor y seguridad" (I, 120).

The state being for Campoamor merely a convenient organization, he has no use for "patriotism," which idealizes the state as a reality having intrinsic existence and value, and which sacrifices humans *de carne y hueso* to what he considers a fictitious entity:

"Ese gran anónimo llamado *patria* es el dios Jagrenat que bajo las les ruedas de su carro suele triturar lo más ilustre que descuella en el mundo por su valor, su virtud y su inteligencia.[1] Los patriotas, sangrientos sacerdotes de una divinidad imaginaria, son los místicos de la profanidad, crean un ídolo de un sueño y adoran su propria demencia; sacrifican mil entes reales ante un fantasma implacable; por respetar una creación, hija desordenada de la fiebre, anulan la naturaleza, que es la encarnación armonizada de Dios" (I, 121).

We have here a typically Iberian manifestation of dislike of the state and a premonition of the anarchist movement. Replying probably to anti-liberal writers such as Jouffroy, who had affirmed that *"L'homme n'a pas de droits, il n'a que des devoirs,"* Campoamor cried:

"¿Cuál debe ser la norma de todas las instituciones? ¿Cada uno para todos? No, señor; todos para cada uno" (I, 122).

Even in his reactionary period, our poet proclaimed his hostility to any exaggerated form of patriotism. In his *Polémicas con la democracia*, he speaks of:

---

[1]"The terrible stories of pilgrims crushed to death in the god's honour have made the phrase 'Car of Juggernaut' synonymous with the merciless sacrifice of human lives, but these have been shown to be baseless calumnies" (*Encyclopaedia Brittanica*, 11th edit., art. Juggernaut).

"Ese diccionario de despropósitos políticos . . . en el cual se llama *patriotismo* al *patrioterismo*" (II, 365).

Whereas he usually condemns patriotism as a form of deceit, Campoamor contradicts himself, or at least seriously complicates his attitude, by exalting patriotism in the chapter "Amor a la patria" of *El personalismo*, where it is described as the highest of earthly loves:

"El amor de la patria es la condensación de todos los amores" (I, 191).

It is proclaimed natural and inevitable:

"El amor de la patria es la ley de gravedad del alma" (I, 191).

In the same passage, cosmopolitanism, despite its intellectual adequacy, is condemned as humanly unsatisfying.

In the chapter "Formas de gobierno" of *El personalismo* (I, 123), Campoamor recognizes the existence of six forms of government: family, tribe, republic, despotism, monarchy and theocracy. He proceeds to study them one by one in the following chapters, iii-viii of Book IV, Section I.

In chapter iii ("Gobierno de familia"), Campoamor develops his favourite idea that the private family has been, is and will be the basis of all societies, past, present, and future. The family is the only pact which is indissoluble because we have drawn it "from the bosom of the Divinity." All the rest of the social structure is arbitrary and conventional.[2]

The "Gobierno de tribu" is summarily dismissed in the following chapter (iv).

In chapter v, the republican form of government is branded with a succession of epigrams. It is described as something slightly better than anarchy:

"La *república* es la madre y el verdugo de todas las virtudes y de todos los vicios. Como Roma arrojaba al circo gladiadores para que se destrozasen mutuamente, la república abre liza a todas las reputaciones para que reciprocamente se exterminen. . . . La rivalidad, el vainén, la lucha son la virilidad de las repúblicas; la tranquilidad, el orden, la atonía son la aurora del despotismo. La salud de las repúblicas es una fiebre remitente. Al populacho la agrada la

---

[2]Campoamor was probably influenced by Victor Hugo's famous *Préface de Cromwell* (1827), which begins with a description of the *temps primitifs*, when man was still in direct contact with God:

"Il y a des familles, et pas de peuples; des pères, et pas de rois. . . . Peu à peu cependant cette adolescence du monde s'en va. Toutes les sphères s'agrandissent; la famille devient tribu, la tribu devient nation."—*Œuvres complètes de Victor Hugo* (Paris: Hetzel, Quantin, n.d.), V, I, 3.

república por la misma razón que a las fieras no les gusta la jaula"
(I, 127).

Such strictures mingled with caresses are not completely unjust. These
criticisms can be aptly applied to any of the three French republics or
to either of the two Spanish ones. Let it be noted that Campoamor
implicitly recognizes the virtues of republicanism. However, he fails
to explain that the difficulty of organizing a republic usually arises from
the circumstances in which it is born. Campoamor was not speaking
with a purely theoretical interest. He was clearly thinking of the Spanish
republican movement, which threatened to destroy law and order in
Spain and, consequently, could have little appeal for a Voltarian epicurean who would thereby lose his job.

Despotism is analysed in the following chapter (vi). The poet's
attitude toward this system of government is happily expressed in the
following metaphor:

> "Los estados despóticos son unos lagos muertos, donde no se reflejan
> más objetos que la imagen del soberano" (I, 129).

Campoamor admits that a nation may flourish under a benevolent
despotism, but affirms that this is a chance, depending upon the character
of the ruler—that is to say, a caprice of fate. It is evident that the
Carlist ideal had no appeal for Campoamor.

In the next chapter (vii), devoted to monarchy, Campoamor aptly
describes the unstable position of monarchy between despotism and
republicanism, with its innumerable varieties falling nearer the one or
the other, a slight propensity to one side opening it to accusations from
the other. The essential quality of monarchy is good faith:

> "El gobierno monárquico-constitucional fundado sobre el recelo es un
> gobierno de engañifas, es un garito público; el mismo gobierno, basado
> sobre la confianza, puede ser el major de los gobiernos" (I, 133).[3]

It must be stressed that when Campoamor talks of a "monarchy" he
means a constitutional monarchy. For him, the ideal was the régime of
Louis Philippe, the fall of which he imputed to an unscrupulous opposition.

Our anti-clerical has not a good word to say for theocracy. He regards
it as a gross abuse of the inherent superstitiousness of mankind. This
immediately evokes a theme common in the writings of his liberal period:
a harsh condemnation of the Roman papacy and a eulogy of Luther as

---

[3]This recalls Montesquieu's belief in the need of virtue in a republic. *Vide L'esprit
des lois*, Book III, chap. iii, "Du principe de la démocratie."

the liberator of the human mind. In view of the reputation Luther enjoys in Spain as in Italy, this idea must have seemed shocking:

"Los ejércitos de la teocracia son ángeles invisibles, sus armas los rayos del cielo, sus delatores las consciencias de los mismos réprobos, sus promesas toda una eternidad de delicias y sus amenazas toda una perpetuidad de dolores. Los pontífices, al empezar diciendo 'En el nombre de Dios . . .' empiezan declarando sus primeros vasallos a los príncipes de la tierra. Para que no se vea nada superior a ellos, los pontífices ciegan los entendimientos con el velo de la fe. . . . Lutero ha sido el Franklin de las teocracias. El último fuego celeste disparado por los pontífices de la tierra vendrá a caer inofensivamente en el parrarayos del libre *examen*" (I, 134).[4]

These words are astounding on the lips of one still officially a member of the Catholic Church. Campoamor displays much more aggressiveness than does Voltaire in the article "Théocratie" of his *Dictionnaire philosophique*.

After enumerating and analysing the various forms of government, Campoamor devotes a chapter to the question "¿Qué forma de gobierno es la mejor?" His answer is that the form of government is indifferent; all can be good or bad. The spirit is the essential, and, in an indirect way, the race:

"La ventura y la estabilidad pueden no hallarse en ninguna forma de gobierno y pueden encontrarse en todas. El buen gobierno muchas veces es como la felicidad: o existe en nosotros o no existe en el mundo; es orgánico en algunas razas como en algunos hombres la felicidad" (I, 136).

The last phrase is connected with Campoamor's race theories, which will be discussed later. In a subsequent passage of *El personalismo*, he expresses the belief that the form of government of a people is a matter of historical contingency and depends, not on the desirability of one type of government, but on the demands of a particular historical situation.

Despite this submissiveness to the force of history, Campoamor does express a very marked preference for the *via media*. On the one hand, he sees the falsity and the danger of the belief in the divine right of kings:

"La soberanía fundada exclusivamente en el derecho divino, que no

---

[4]Franklin's dual role as scientist and politican made this type of comparison a commonplace of the late eighteenth and early nineteenth century. *"Eripuit caelo fulmen sceptrumque tyrannis"* was the expression universally applied to Franklin. *Vide* Sydney George Fisher, *The True Benjamin Franklin* (Philadelphia: J. B. Lippincott, 1899), 309ff.

es más que el prestigio de la tradición, es una usurpación de todo lo individual, de todo lo inteligente, de todo lo divino. Es una ab- dicación de la libertad, una protesta contra el libre albedrío, una negación de la personalidad, es detestar contra el objeto de la *na- turaleza*, es dejar inútil la obra de Dios" (I, 145).

This remark is undoubtedly aimed at the Carlists. Campoamor would probably argue that reason, as well as a modicum of divine right, was on the side of Isabel II.

However, the dangers on the left excite our anti-revolutionary more than the dangers on the right. Despite his liberalism, he uses the lan- guage of a reactionary to express his Volterian opinion of universal suffrage. He tells us that universal suffrage establishes as directors of the state the idiocy and inertia of demagogy, which gravitates toward barbarity as lead toward the earth. Continuing, Campoamor declares that universal suffrage buries the spirit under the weight of the flesh, substitutes a public which is noble, because of its personality, by a number of anonymous entities; that it is the mutilation of the people who read, write, judge, and think; that it is the hecatomb of all the aristocracies conquered by work, by virtue, and by intelligence (I, 147).

Our poet's references to universal suffrage are equalled in potency only by those he makes to the Spanish Republicans' copy of "*Liberté, Egalité, Fraternité*":

"Acometamos de frente esa ciudadela del error, donde se parapetan los pseudo-filántropos, los falsos patriotas y los mentidos liberales, y rompamos esa bandera donde están escritas las palabras *libertad, igualdad, fraternidad*; consigna que desde la revolución francesa está siendo la enseña de una *libertad* que es la más soez de las tiranías, de una *igualdad* que es una hedionda mescolanza y de una *fraternidad* que es la apoteosis del cainismo" (I, 147-48).

In this great social barrier to progress and human dignity, where then lies the narrow gate? It would seem to be through aristocracy, to which Campoamor devotes an enthusiastic panegyric. Now an aris- tocracy is much more typical of a monarchy than of a despotism or a republic, so that, despite his statement that the choice depends upon historical contingency, Campoamor's preference for monarchies is once more evident:

"Yo soy aristócrata hasta la adoración. . . . No conozco un solo gobierno aristocrático que no sea enérgico, inteligente y tenaz, mientras que en la historia de la humanidad no hallo un solo acto

de la muchedumbre que no sea o una extravagancia o una repro-
bación" (I, 152).

It would be uncharitable to suggest that Campoamor's "adoration" of
aristocracy was partly inspired by his own desire to emphasize his
proclaimedly genteel origin. The one-act play *Dies Irae* (1873) purports
to be a picture of the struggle between the aristocracy and the people in
sixteenth-century Germany, but in reality it is an indictment of communistic attacks on the aristocracy. A significant speech is that of the
protagonist, Count Tello de Quirós, which begins:

"¡Comunistas absolutos, juzgad vuestras doctrinas por los frutos!"
(VI, 257).

Although Campoamor was loud in his praise of Luther and the religious
revolution, he was equally vehement in his condemnation of the accompanying social upheaval.

Campoamor's attitude toward liberalism is rather childish; it is
subordinated entirely to the aristocractic principle:

"¡Qué liberal era yo cuando aún no lo era la plebe! . . . En España
eran liberales los caballeros cuanto era la plebe servil; después que
la plebe se fué liberalizando, los caballeros fueron transigiendo con
las ideas realistas" (I, 335).

Again, Campoamor is striving to insinuate that he was of aristocratic
birth.

Not only did Campoamor cease to be a liberal; during his reactionary
period, he developed a hostility to any attempt to modify society. It is
curious that this ossified and obscurantist conservatism should coincide,
by its appeal to hypothetical natural laws of society, with the pure
liberal theory of government. In *Lo absoluto*, there is an almost pathetic
exhortation:

"¡Economistas! ¡Socialistas! ¡Igualitarios! ¡Comunistas! hijos de la
ignorancia y hermanos todos del crimen, dejadnos gozar, si gozamos
tranquilamente; y, si sufrimos, dejadnos sufrir el dolor en paz y en
gracia de Dios. Hay leyes sociales naturales, como hay leyes naturales para las demás obras de la creación" (I, 627).

The worst offenders are apparently economists![5] Campoamor's request
to be allowed to suffer in peace and in the grace of God is decidedly

---

[5]It must be remembered that, in the nineteenth century, economists were often
regarded with suspicion and were the object of a papal encyclical. *Vide* René Gonnard,
Histoire des doctrines économiques (Paris: Valois, 1930).

fatalistic and truly Iberian. In *Polémicas con la democracia*, there is
another exposition of Campoamor's reactionary laissez faire theory. If,
he asks, Athens, Phoenicia, Carthage, Rome, Venice, and Greece have
reached great prosperity by natural growth without the guidance of
economic theories, why should not the nations of today achieve well-
being without the interference of theorists? (II, 423-24). This argument
sounds strangely familiar.

Campoamor, who, in his liberal period, had laughed at the university
which had deplored *"la funesta manía de pensar,"* came close to adopting
this attitude in his indictment of democracy. He blamed philosophers
for all the deep unrest in the world:

> "Las verdaderas revoluciones las hacen sólo los filósofos . . . los
> políticos no promueven más que los motines . . . no basta sólo que
> se sostenga el orden en los hechos; es necesario también no permitir
> que se introduzca el desorden en las ideas" (II, 364).

Campoamor's reactionary development provoked a deep resentment
among his former liberal companions, who branded him a turncoat, just
as Browning reproached Wordsworth. The most marked bitterness was
between our poet and Castelar, who, in his *Fórmula del progreso* (1857),[6]
declared that alone the democratic party offered promise of betterment
for Spain; Campoamor replied by constantly making Castelar the butt
of his irony in *Polémicas con la democracia*. The orator, with sangiune
optimism, announced that, despite a few passing setbacks, democracy
would finally triumph the whole world over, and ironically warned
Campoamor that he would have to flee to a desert in Africa. The poet
reacted in a puerile fashion and devoted three pages to developing the
theme *"Adiós, que me voy a Africa!"* (II, 537-540).

Another participant in this dispute was Nemesio Fernández Cuesta y
Picatoste (1818-1893), an outstanding journalist of nineteenth-century
Spain. In 1854 he founded *El Adelanto*, which was soon transformed
into *La Discusión*, one of the great newspapers of the period. Fernández
Cuesta was its editor, while the staff included Rivero, Martos, Manuel del
Palacio, Bastemeti, Pi, who later became the editor, and Castelar, who
was also the founder and editor of *La Democracia*. In order to confound
both *La Democracia* and *La Discusión*, Campoamor created the periodical
El Estado, in which he published most of the articles later gathered
together under the title *Polémicas con la democracia*. *El Estado* seems
to have had a very short life.

---

[6]The most common edition of the *Fórmula del progreso* is that of 1870. The first
edition seems to have appeared in 1857, although the *Espasa* and other authorities,
probably through an error, say 1867.

Fernández Cuesta published a pamphlet in support of Castelar. It was refuted by the Conde de Torres Cabrera[7] in an article which Campoamor did not see, and by Enrique O'Donnell,[8] who *"en otro folleto escrito con una elegancia y una elevación notables, se puso de parte de las ideas de orden"* (II, 379). Campoamor admits that he does not know O'Donnell, but thanks him sincerely for his efforts on behalf of *"la buena causa."*[9]

Canalejas entered the lists and addressed to our reactionary a letter which the latter, with an implied reference to Canalejas' French liberalism and Germanic philosophy, describes as *galo-germánica.* Much to the poet's irritation, the democratic paper *La Discusión* praised the letter for its *"severidad del raciocinio,"* its *"hermosura de la dicción"* and its *"variedad del estilo."*

The economist Gabriel Rodríguez[10] published a similar attack on Campoamor, which *La Discusión* qualified as *"muy correcta en su estilo."* The poet replied with annoyed impatience that *"no viene al caso."*

The intricate history of Spanish political parties is a nightmare for Hispanists, and it is no surprise to find that a representative of a third party entered the arena and attacked both the combatants: Carlos Rubio published a pamphlet entitled *La teoría del progreso* on behalf of the Partido Progresista.[11] However, our reactionary thought that here was

---

[7]Ricardo Martel y Fernández de Córdoba (1832-1912), ninth Count of Torres Cabrera, was prominent socially, but has left practically no trace as a writer.

[8]Enrique O'Donnell y Jorris (died 1869), a general of few literary pretensions, should not be confused with his more famous brother Leopoldo, Conde de Lucena and Duque de Tetuán (1809-1867), with General Enrique José O'Donnell (1769-1834), one of the heroes of the War of Independence, or with his nephew, Carlos O'Donnell y Abren (1834-1903), second Duke of Tetuán. Enrique O'Donnell, himself, wrote *Apuntes históricos sobre la familia de O'Donnell* (Madrid, 1868).

[9]This is Campoamor's version of the story, which is somewhat garbled. It was Enrique O'Donnell who published at Madrid in 1858 a reply to Castelar's *Fórmula del progreso* entitled *La democracia española.* This was refuted in its turn by Fernández Cuesta, in his *Vindicación de la democracia española. Contestación al folleto de D. E. O'Donnell* (1858). The real order is Castelar-O'Donnell-Fernández Cuesta, whereas Campoamor inverts the last two.

[10]Gabriel Rodríguez (1827-1901) was one of the most active economists of nineteenth-century Spain. An advocate of free-trade, he was one of the founders of the Asociación para la Reforma de los Aranceles y Aduanas. He was a militant member of the Ateneo and took part in practically all the polemics of his time. *Vide* Rodríguez y Villalonga, *Gabriel Rodríguez* (Madrid, 1917).

[11]Carlos Rubio y Collet (1832-1871), a perennial member of the *Partido Progresista*, published in 1859 the opuscule to which Campoamor is referring, *Teoría del progreso: folleto escrito en contestación al que con el título de 'La fórmula del progreso' ha publicado don Emilio Castelar.* This was in addition to his articles in *La Iberia*, in which he likewise attacked Castelar very severely.

an ally rather than an enemy and greeted him warmly. The chaotic warfare crystallized into a struggle of *El Estado* and *La Iberia* against *La Democracia* and *La Discusión*.

A number of other less noteworthy attacks on Campoamor were published. Feeling that he, the representative of the Partido Moderado (as he claimed to be), was the target of a concerted attack from the Partido Democrático, the poet ironically suggested that a scheme existed to adapt to real life and more precisely to his life the comedy *Llueven bofetones* (II, 398).

Campoamor, a few years later, in 1864, found himself confronted, not with individuals, but with an army. Thirty prominent Democrats convened and issued a manifesto. The leader of the group and the first to sign the manifesto was Francisco Pí y Margall. The most notable absentees were Castelar, who, as a professor, was afraid of losing his chair, and Nicolás María Rivero, who did not take part in this demonstration, for some reason which Campoamor could not imagine. The manifesto read as follows:

> "Con el deseo de evitar toda división del partido democrático que pudiera proceder de un concepto equivocado, varios amigos nuestros se reunieron y han acordado hacer la manifestación que a continuación insertamos. Los que subscriben declaran que consideran como demócratas indistintamente a todos aquellos que, cualesquiera que sean sus opiniones en filosofía y en cuestiones económicas y sociales profesan en política el principio de la personalidad humana o de las libertades individuales, absolutas e ilegislables y el del sufragio universal, así como los demás principios políticos fundamentales, consignados en el programa democrático."[12]

Campoamor proceeds to discuss this program at considerable length and attempts to prove that it means nothing. However, these ideas have little intrinsic value; the interest of this episode is purely historical.

---

[12]Pí y Margall, who was later to be President of the First Spanish Republic, became in 1864 director of *La Discusión*, in which he defended socialism and attacked individualistic democrats. This provoked a conflict within his own Partido Democrático, many of whose members were either defenders of individualism or anti-socialist. It was in order to counteract the latent schism that Pí obtained the *Declaración de los Treinta*.

CHAPTER VII

PHILOSOPHY OF HISTORY

THE theory of progress and even of perfectability was fundamental in that philosophy of history which is considered typical of the eighteenth century. However, Campoamor, in his most liberal work *El personalismo*, devotes a chapter entitled "Perfectibilidad humana" (III, viii) to refuting this idea. He asks Condorcet what he means when he says that man can perfect himself infinitely.[1] What does "infinitely" mean? Campoamor rightly points out that man's sphere of action is limited and that his freedom is best described in the remark that man is as free as a bird in its cage (I, 93). It is possible that Campoamor is following Voltaire, who did not share his century's belief in unending progress. It is more probable that he is being consonant with the Hispanic traditional belief, reinforced by the Romantic movement, in the limits placed by Fate upon the individual. However, Campoamor is quite un-Spanish in his application of his criterion of intelligence to the question of progress:

"El hombre sólo es perfectible en el grado que es inteligente" (I, 94). Campoamor does not deny the existence of progress, which, over long periods, he considers to be evident. The court of Louis XIV was superior to that of Clovis, the military ability of Napoleon was greater than that of Attila. Yet even such progress seems doubtful to Campoamor. After quoting some thirteen examples of human advancement, he enumerates a like number of cases of retrogression, some of which seem to our ears decidedly amusing. Our optimist concludes that it is doubtful whether man is happier today than he was in Adam's time; in any case, sorrow (*el dolor*), is always with us.

Campoamor has not expressed any definite opinions on the then-burning question of mechanical progress, but he relates an episode which reveals a half-frightened, half-curious attitude toward engineering. He was a member of the royal party led by Isabel II, which travelled on the official train inaugurating the railroad from Madrid to Alicante, built

---

[1]Campoamor is referring chiefly to Condorcet's *Esquisse d'un tableau historique des progrès de l'esprit humain* (1795), which had an enormous success; the Convention bought three thousand copies and distributed them throughout France. In the Introduction, Condorcet explains the fundamental idea of his work:

"Qu'il n'a été marqué aucun terme au perfectionnement des facultés humaines; que la perfectibilité de l'homme est réellement indéfinie; que les progrès de cette perfectibilité, désormais indépendants de toute puissance qui voudrait les arrêter, n'ont d'autre terme que la durée du globe où la nature nous a jetés."

by the Marqués de Salamanca.[2] Campoamor relates, in *Polémicas con la democracia* (II, 648), the passage of the train through Monóvar, Novelda, Monforte, Agost, San Vicente, and the other villages on the route. A special thrill awaited the party at Rambla de Elda[3]:

"Al llegar al puente que se llama de la rambla de Elda recibimos un obsequio del señor Salamanca, que no le hemos agradecido. Nuestros lectores habrán oído hablar de un puente alto, muy alto, que los viajeros procuran pasar dormidos para tener el gusto de no verle. Pues bien: encima de aquel puente alto, muy alto, que marea el verlo hasta a los mismos que no se marean en alta mar, tuvo el señor Salamanca la feliz occurencia, que le agradeceremos que no se repita, de parar el tren para que contemplásemos la belleza y seguridad de la obra. El puente es muy bello desde arriba, pero de seguro nos hubiera parecido mucho más agradable desde abajo."

At Alicante, the locomotives were blessed by a prelate. Our poet repeatedly suggests, in a half-serious fashion, that, in railroad locomotives, the devil has been enchained. He relates how, after the blessing:

"Nuestras terribles conversas lanzaron a compás y retrocediendo algunos pasos un grito agudo, como si en aquel momento el espíritu de Satanás, espantado del exorcismo, saliese de las entrañas de aquellas nuevas vírgenes de fundición, dejándolas incólumes de todo pecado y libras de todo mal pensamiento ulterior de romper la crisma a algún infeliz viajero que en el porvenir se entregue a su inteligente dirección y a su moderna religiosidad" (II, 649).

This narrative is picturesque and interesting, but it does not reveal in Campoamor any belief in mechanical progress.

Our poet could not believe in progress as an automatic phenomenon, since he held that humanity is carried forward by a few great men. This idea is reminiscent of Carlylian hero-worship, but there is nothing to suggest that the Spaniard had read the works of the Englishman. In *El personalismo* (I, 101), Campoamor declares that the history of civiliza-

[2]José de Salamanca y Mayol (1811-1883), the most famous financier of nineteenth-century Spain, was made a grandee with the title Conde de los Llanos y Marqués de Salamanca. He is usually designated by the latter title. It was chiefly through his inspiration that most of the railroads of Spain were built. The opening of the line from Madrid to Alicante was a historic event, since it was the first to join the capital and the coast. The development of Spanish railroads during this period is described in Pedro de Répide, *Isabel II, Reina de España* (in series "Vidas españolas e hispano-americanas del siglo XIX"; Madrid: Espasa-Calpe, 1932).

[3]Elda is a village in the province of Alicante, diocesis of Orihuela and *partido judicial* of Manóvar. It is situated on the left bank of the River Vinalapó.

tion can be reduced to the biography of not more than two dozen men; that the habits, the ideas, and the principles of the mass of mankind are poor imitations and pale reflections of these twenty-four personalities; that every progressive initiative, and consequently every historical honor belong exclusively to genius, to the most "intimately personal" thing which exists. This rather arresting expression reveals the relationship between the hero-worship of Campoamor and his cult of *El personalismo*. With a happy metaphor, the poet declares that:

"Lo mismo en el orden moral que en el intelectual, que en el político, cada grande hombre es una palanca de Arquimedes" (I, 140).

Campoamor's hero-worship is reflected in his concept of the social hierarchy. Although he limits the number of great men in history to twenty-four, whom the rest of mankind have imitated, nevertheless he creates in society a class of so-called *notables*; apparently they are the raw-material for heroes:

"Los hombres, según la mayor o menor *cantidad* de su inteligencia, se dividen en tres clases: *vulgares, discretos y notables*. Los primeros, por ley natural, han nacido para obedecer, los segundos para obedecer o mandar en puestos subalternos y los terceros para mandar en primer término" (I, 138).

It is interesting to note that, even in the question of ordering and obeying, Campoamor makes intelligence his sole criterion.

Since history can be reduced to the biography of less than two dozen men, it is for Campoamor an inversion and a total distortion of realty to write a general history in which great men are allotted their place in the total development of humanity. Our hero-worshipper therefore witnessed with dismay and indignation the growth of scientific history. He described it, in *El personalismo*, as a modern invention, more pernicious and more opiatic for personal emulation, and thus for history, than the Indian Vedantism imported by Spinoza (I, 101). As an individualist, he objected to the dissolution of his own personality, as well as that of the great men of the past, in a general historical development, and protested:

"Eso de que me entierren vivo en el inmenso sarcófago de mi especie me causa una repugnancia invencible" (id.).

Besides its destruction of human values, Campoamor accused history of an inevitable distortion. He recalls the story of Alexander who, on hearing a narration of his exploits, asked Lysimachus, "Where was I when those fine deeds were done?" He compares history with popular attraction at the fairs of his day; namely, a room containing a thousand mirrors in which objects were reflected large or small, and black or white[?], according to the position from which they were viewed.

What greater or more wilful distortion of facts, asks Campoamor, than the so-called philosophy of history? With Volterian scepticism, he devotes the chapter "Filosofía de la historia" of *El personalismo* (Book III, x) to analyzing the historical philosophy of the most outstanding representatives of this "science": Bossuet, Vico, Herder, Hegel, Condorcet, Schlegel, Hoene-Wronski,[4] and Count A. Cieszkowski.[5] This chapter makes interesting and convincing reading, for the concatenation of summaries certainly gives the impression that facts can be found to support any conceivable philosophy of history. Moreover, says Campoamor, this "science" is naïve in its pompous affirmation of truisms. He ridicules Vico on this account in the *dolora* "La ciencia nueva de Vico." A schoolmaster explains at length to a small village group the division of history into three periods by Vico:[6]

"'O vuestro Vico es un tonto,
o yo no sé qué pensar'
dijo al maestro de pronto
el sacristán del lugar.
no es gran mérito el zurcir
la historia de esa manera;
nacer, crecer y morir . . . .
eso lo sabe cualquiera' " (V, 225).

In his *discurso de entrada* in the Academia de la Historia, Menéndez y Pelayo maintained that biassed history is more interesting than true history[7]:

"La historia es grande, bella e interesante, no porque el historiador sea *imparcial*, sino al revés, por su *parcialidad* manifiesta."

Campoamor, with his realistic dislike of the distortion of facts, retorted in *El idealismo* that only his admiration and liking for Menéndez y Pelayo prevented his taking vengeance for the unpleasant reference to himself in the *Historia de los heterodoxos españoles*,[8] and telling Don Marcelino

---

[4]Josef Marja Hoene-Wronski (1778-1858), Polish philosopher. *Vide* S. Dickstein, *Hoene-Wronski* (Cracow, 1896); Christian Cherfils, *Introduction à Wronski, philosophe et réformateur* (Paris: Fischbacher, 1898).

[5]August Cieszkowski (1814-1894), a Polish disciple of Hegel. *Vide* A. Zoltowski, *Graf A. Cieszkowski's Philosophie der Tot, Grundzuge seiner Lehre und der Aufbau seines Systems* (Posnan, 1904).

that, if the idea were accepted, the Academy would be officially converted into a workshop for producing lies (III, 501-2). Fortunately, Campoamor's fears proved vain, and the Academia de la Historia continued to be probably the most scholarly and the most active of the Academies. However, for reasons which we can well understand, it had nothing to offer to Campoamor.

---

[6]For the bibliography of this subject, *vide* B. Croce, *Bibliografia vichiana* (1904-1936); Croce himself takes Vico more seriously than does Campoamor. *Vide* B. Croce, *La filosofia di Giambattista Vico* (3rd edit., Bari, 1933).

[7]Menéndez y Pelayo became a member of the Academia de la Historia in 1883. The theme of his *discurso* was "La Historia como arte bello." A description of the occasion is to be found in Luis Antón del Olmet y Arturo García Carraffa, *Menéndez Pelayo* (Madrid: Juan Pueyo, 1913), chap. xii. Campoamor somewhat distorts the ideas of Don Marcelino.

[8]*Vide supra.*

CHAPTER VIII

RACE THEORY

THERE is a fundamental difference between Campoamor's concept of the nations of the world and that of Pardo-Bazán. The woman travelled widely and interpreted her impressions with the help of books. The man scarcely left the Peninsula except for a trip to England and had a purely academic acquaintance with the civilization of other countries. One of his idiosyncracies was a quaint hatred of travel. He professed, in a semi-serious way, not to believe in the existence of China or Mexico, "*países inventados por los geógrafos noveleros*."[1]

This bookish knowledge of the peoples of the earth explains in part Campoamor's arrangement of them into a rigid, almost mathematical hierarchy. As we shall see, however, by comparing Campoamor's ideas with those of modern anthropologists, he was surprisingly well informed on the subject. His fundamental division of mankind is into four races: white (*blanca*), yellow (*amarilla*), copper-colored (*cobriza*), and black (*negra*). "*Raza cobriza*" designates the natives of America.[2] It is chiefly in *El personalismo* that Campoamor develops in detail his views about the constituent parts of humanity. He tells us that, in every epoch and in all latitudes, the white begets white, the Malayan Malayans, and the negro negroes; that races have an organic and constitutional type, which neither invasions nor commerce can eradicate (I, 72-73). This belief in the race as the dominant factor in mankind coincides with the modern race theory, although Campoamor had read neither Gobineau[3] nor Gumplovicz.[3]

---

[1]Andrés González Blanco, *Campoamor*, 192-93.

[2]The two principal defects of this classification are, firstly, that Campoamor considers as a race apart the American aborigines, and tends to group them with the negroes, never suggesting a relationship with the yellow race; and, secondly, that he fails to mention races of doubtful classification (Australian, Vedda, Irula, Kolarians, Moi, Senoi, Toala, etc.). Otherwise, his grouping coincides with that of outstanding contemporary anthropologists such as A. L. Kroeber, who recognizes three primary stocks: Caucasian or white, mongoloid or yellow, and negroid or black. Kroeber's subdivision of these stocks is different from that of Campoamor. *Vide* A. L. Kroeber, *Anthropology* (New York: Harcourt Brace, 1923), 41. It is interesting to note that two competent anthropologists such as Luis de Hoyos Sáinz and Telesforo de Avanzadi, in their *Lecciones de antropología* (1900), III and IV, still follow Campoamor's quadruple division.

[3]Dates are important here. It is just possible, but not probable, that Campoamor had seen Gobineau's *Essai sur l'inégalité des races humaines* (1853), which appeared two years before *El personalismo;* in it Gobineau affirmed that there are superior and

Campoamor did not believe in the community of origin of races. He protested indignantly when Cesare Cantù[4] attempted to prove that the similarity of language reveals a historical identity of races (I, 236). Cantù was comparing the Indo-European languages and attempting to establish a community of origin merely for the Ayran peoples. It would seem, therefore, that Campoamor refused to accept the theory of a common origin, not only for the four races of mankind, but also for the subdivisions of the races.[5]

Campoamor changed in his ideas regarding the influence of climate. At first, he attributed everything to race, but, as he became more conservative, he realized that to place emphasis upon Aryanism was equivalent to humiliating the Mediterranean nations, including Spain, and he increasingly emphasized the importance of climate. In his *Filosofía de las leyes*, which in other respects follows Montesquieu closely, he rejects the theories of the *philosophe* concerning the influence of climate (I, 271ff.). Later, in *El idetsmo*, he expresses approval of these same ideas of Montesquieu (III, 532). In order to prove these theories, he twice[6] affirms that English families, when they migrate to India, cease to have fair children.[7]

Campoamor's racial theories are not disinterested and scientific. They resemble the modern brand in that they are above all a basis for discrimination. The criterion which Campoamor uses in establishing a hierarchy of peoples is the same as he employs for the members of a society: namely, *inteligencia* and *personalidad*. Indeed, he establishes a parallel between the social and the racial hierarchy, in both cases refuting the partisans of equality. Nature, he says, has made peoples, just as it has made individuals, unequal in the quantity of their intelligence.

inferior races, and that the majority of races are incapable of civilization. Gobineau had a flock of imitators, including Lapouge, Ammon, and Chamberlain.

[4]Campoamor is referring to the *Storia universale* (1836-1847) of Cesare Cantù (1804-1895). The *Storia universale* had an astonishing success.

[5]This question has been the great bone of contention of anthropologists. The monogenists, such as Blumenbach, Cuvier, Pritchard, Waitz and Quatrefages, group all races together under Linneus' label, *homo sapiens*. The polygenists, such as Heine, Rudolphi, Virey, Morton and Broca recognize the existence of various human species, from two, white man and black man (Virey), to fifteen (Bory de Saint-Vincent). *Vide* Manuel Antón y Ferrándiz, *Antropología* (Madrid: Sucesores de Rivadeneyra, 1912), chap. ii, "Monogenismo y poligenismo." The actuality of this question in Campoamor's time is shown in A. de Quatrefages, *Unité de l'espèce humaine* (Paris: Hachette, 1861).

[6]*La metafísica y la poesía*, III, 406; *El ideísmo*, III, 532.

[7]This is quite wrong. Kroeber says:

"*Hair color* and *eye color* are practically immune against direct change by environment. They unquestionably are excellent hereditary criteria" (*Anthropology*, 40).

He draws three comparisons between the two hierarchies. The negroes and the copper-colored are "*los proletarios*" of the state, the Asiatics are "*los menestrales*," and the Europeans are "*los patricios.*" The first are children, the second youths, and the third adults. The first represent instinct, the second perception, the third reason (I, 75).

The hierarchy of the four races of mankind is, beginning from the bottom, the black, the copper-colored, the yellow and the white. From this basis, Campoamor developed a theory which is at least ingenious: namely, that the fairer the skin of a people, the higher it is in the hierarchy of races.[8] If this theory is applied to the white race, it accords the highest rank to the flaxen-haired peoples of northern Europe and relegates the swarthy Mediterranean type to second place. In his liberal period, Campoamor was faithful to the implications of his theory, and idolized the English, particularly those of Norman, i.e. Scandinavian origin; nonetheless, he constantly accused the Germans of being oriental-ized. Among the dark Mediterranean peoples, he placed the French, sprinkled with blondness, just below the English and was content to accept an inferior position for the olive-skinned Spaniards. In his reactionary period, such an order was naturally repugnant to him and, in refusing to accept it any longer, he dealt a death-blow to his whole color theory.

Any philosophy concerning the hierarchy of races, describing some as inherently superior, others as permanently inferior, must clash, in Campoamor's time as now, with the universality of the Catholic Church. Our anti-clerical anthropologist realized this danger and countered it, in *El personalismo*, with a eulogy of the universality of the Church:

"Yo nunca admiraré bastante la grandeza de ese templo, donde caben en conjunto todas las razas humanas, pasadas, presentes y futuras" (I, 261).

There is an interesting mixture of admiration and irony in this panegyric:

"En él [el templo cristiano], los habitantes de Africa pueden adorar *fetiques* de madera, los oceánicos serpientes simbólicas, los asiáticos fuegos sagrados, los americanos [*the Indians, of course*] reliquias antimaléficas, los europeos, si son artistas y amantes de lo objetivo, de la naturaleza externa, pueden admirar catedrales, cuadros, estatuas, procesiones cuya riqueza es oriental y cuyo gusto es ex-quisito [*This sounds ironical when we recall Campoamor's dislike of cathedrals and his hatred of the Orient*]; y si los europeos son filósofos,

---

[8]The preference for blonds goes back at least to Greek times. *Vide* J. B. Bury, *History of Greece* (London: Macmillan, 1902), I, 37, footnote.

amantes de lo subjetivo, de la naturaleza interna, entonces pueden admirar la moral de Cristo, terciar con los nominalistas y los realistas [*When we think of Campoamor's scorn for these theological squabbles, we cannot believe that he is completely serious*]" (I, 262).

Embracing all the races of the earth, the Catholic Church can take in all its social strata:

"El catolicismo . . . . sequirá prodigando a los *aristócratas* del espíritu, misterios, abstracción, espiritualismo; a la *mesocracia*, sermones, racionalismo, doctrina; a la *democracia*, procesiones, músicas y perdones" (I, 263).

Campoamor is clearly attempting to reproduce traditional eulogies of the catholicism of the Church. Although Campoamor has in this way paid lip-service to Rome, the implication throughout this passage is that the Church is not discriminating, and, for our aristocratic philosopher, discrimination is an essential quality.

THE HIERARCHY OF RACES, ACCORDING TO CAMPOAMOR

The scale reads upwards. Notice that it becomes increasingly complex.

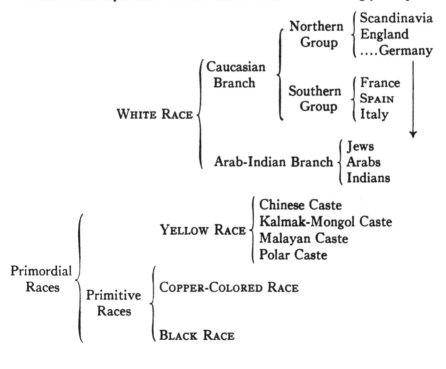

CHAPTER IX

THE PRIMORDIAL RACES

CAMPOAMOR groups the black, the copper-colored, and the yellow races together under the adjective "primordial," as opposed to the superior white race. Gobineau would have been pleased at the impatient scorn with which the Spaniard dismisses the "primordial" races. In *El personalismo*, Campoamor affirms:

"En el inmenso territorio que ocupan las tres razas primordiales, *negra, cobreza* y *amarilla*, y las mezclas que se derivan de ellas, no hay un solo país donde exista un gobierno tolerable: o es la república de las fieras, donde triunfa el que puede más, o es la monarquía del león, que vence porque puede más" (I, 143).

In the chapter "Raza negra" of *El personalismo* (Book III, iii), our Spaniard gives a damning account of the black race, whose utter primitiveness is the leitmotif of the description:

"Aun causa rubor llamarlos hombres" (I, 76).

Campoamor did not realize, as do modern anthropologists, that there is a complete diversity among negro tribes. He says nothing about the strict sense of honesty and justice which characterizes many African groups.[1] Although a liberal, he saw nothing reprehensible in slavery, which, he says, negroes accept without protest.[2] He condemns several tribes, such as the Hottentots, because they are no use even as slaves.[3] Not the slightest ray of hope shines in this gloomy picture of the Dark Continent.

Within the primordial races, Campoamor groups together the black and the copper-colored races, as representing the lowest possible stage of humanity. The "Raza cobriza" is described in Book III, chapter iv, of *El personalismo*. Campoamor places it slightly higher than the black race, but he is doubtful whether he should make this distinction,

---

[1] *Vide* C. G. Seligman, *Races of Africa* ("Home University Library"; London: Thornton Butterworth, 1930): Dietrich Westermann, *The African To-Day* (International Institute of African Languages and Cultures: Oxford University Press, 1934).

[2] *Vide* Gabriel Rodríguez, "La idea y el movimiento anti-exclavistas en España durante el Siglo XIX," *La España del Siglo XIX, colección de conferencias históricas* [held in the Ateneo] (Madrid: Antonio San Martín, 1887), III, 321-355.

[3] *Vide The Early Cape Hottentots, described in the writings of Olfert Dapper (1668), Willem Ten Rhyne (1686) and Johannes Gulielmus de Grevenbroek (1695)* (edit., I. Schapera and B. Farrington; Cape Town: Van Riebeeck Society, 1933).

since Ulloa[4] and Venegas[5] describe the Indians as idiotic and affirm that the negro slaves, who showed a much greater aptitude for work, considered themselves to belong to a superior race. As for the American Indians of today, Campoamor says that it is uncertain if they are reasonable beings (I, 79). The only Indian tribes for which he can find the slightest admiration are the Iroquois and the Araucanians, whose fierce bravery is truly epic (I, 73).

Campoamor, who grouped the copper-colored with the negro race, never once suspected that it was in any way related to the yellow peoples. He cannot be blamed for this, since the theory is not perfectly satisfactory and is still rejected by a few.[6]

When our wit made the aforementioned remark that he did not believe in Mexico or China, he was really referring to the fabulous civilizations which have been the object of so many descriptions. Campoamor had a healthy suspicion of exotism. He was endowed with enough common sense to resist the wave of Orientalophilia which swept Europe in the second half of the nineteenth century, for he saw all the misery hidden behind the baroque facade. In the same way, he rejected the colorful descriptions of Pre-Columbian civilization to which chroniclers have accustomed us.   He condemns *"las orientalescas exageraciones de todos los historiadores de España"* (I, 79).

Campoamor hated the Orient.   He warned Europe of a "yellow peril": he considered Asia as a land of inertia (Japan had not yet emerged from its cocoon), and he feared that its spiritual immobility might infect European civilization.   He accused, as germ-carriers, German philosophers who indulged in abstract speculation, and who had lost all vitality and sense of action:

"Si con los ojos en el principio absoluto véis con imperturbable indiferencia el exterminio universal del mundo externo, llegaréis a asiatizar al género humano, convirtiendo en inercia todo principio

---

[4]Campoamor is evidently referring to the *Noticias americanas* (Madrid, 1772) of Antonio de Ulloa, who, however, does not paint as dark a picture of the Indians as Campoamor suggests.

[5]Miguel Venegas (1680-1764), *Noticia de la California* (Madrid: M. Fernández, 1757). It should be remembered that the Californian Indian represented one of the lowest types.

[6]*Vide The American Aborigines. Their Origin and Antiquity*, edit., Diamond Jenness (University of Toronto Press, 1933). The first real exponent of the theory of the immigration of the American aborigines from northeastern Asia was Johannes de Laet, a Dutchman who quarreled with his compatriot Hugo de Groot (Grotius) because Grotius, in his *Disertatio de origine gentium Americanarum* (1643), proposed many other explanations of the peopling of America.

de actividad, y le avezaréis, por último, a permanecer constantemente en éxtasis, como los indios, mirándose inmóvil la punta de la nariz" (I, 30-31).

By his cult of action and vital, as opposed to abstract, and static thought, Campoamor was indeed a son of the romantic movement. It is ironical that the Germans, through the mouth of Kaiser Wilhelm II, should declare themselves the defenders of Europe against a "yellow peril" which was just the antithesis of the one denounced by Campoamor.

In the chapter "Raza amarilla" of *El personalismo* (Book III, v), Campoamor divides the yellow race into four "castes":

"La raza amarilla abraza cuatro castas distintas: la *polar*, tan sucia como ruin, la *malaca*, muy aviesa, la *calmuco-mongola*, sumamente tosca, y la *china*, en extremo suave" (I, 82).[7]

This use of the word "caste" is peculiar to Campoamor's philosophy. He wishes thereby to indicate not merely the difference between human groups, but also their place in the racial hierarchy he establishes.

In the "*casta polar*," which is a not unsatisfactory term invented apparently by Campoamor, are included, principally, the Lapps, Samoyads, Ostyaks, Tungus, Kamchadeles, and "*zemblios*." What tribe Campoamor places in Novaya Zemlia is a mystery. He does not mention the Eskimos, who would seem well-qualified to belong to the "Polar Caste." Campoamor includes, then, in his "*casta polar*" roughly the northern half of the northern Mongols. He says that they are "*menguado en su físico y abjecto en su moral*" (I, 82). He is right in both details; Keane gives the average height as less than 5' 6" and says that they are "dull, reserved, somewhat sullen and apathetic" (p. 266). Keane makes a reservation for the Tungus, asserting that "All observers speak in enthusiastic language of the temperament and moral qualities of the Tunguses" (p. 288); Campoamor fails to make any such distinction and does not mention the Finns, who are an even more notable exception. What he does with them (as with the related Magyars and Bulgars) is

[7]A. H. Keane, in *Man, Past and Present* (Cambridge University Press, 1900) establishes (p. 171) the following division for the yellow race:
        1) Mongolo-Tartar
          (Northern Mongols)
Homo Mongolicus
        2) a) Tibeto-Indo-Chinese b) Oceanic Mongols
          (Southern Mongols)
Campoamor's classification differs in that he divides the northern Mongols into a "*casta polar*" and a "*casta calmucomongola*," and classifies the Japanese and Koreans with the southern Monguls rather than with the northern Mongols.

not clear. It seems as though he is avoiding mention of them and their relatively high degree of civilization in order to facilitate his theory concerning the inherent and permanent hierarchy of races. Admittedly the so-called Turanians are something of a mystery.[8]

Rising one step in the ethnological scale established by Campoamor, we come to the *"casta malaca,"* the Malays, or oceanic Mongols, as they are often called. Our European thought that they were essentially rogues (I, 73). He affirms, in *El personalismo:*

"Las islas del mar del Sur, pobladas por la rama malays, forman el arrabal o barrio bajo del mundo, pues los indígenas que las habitan son la casta más acanallada y aviesa del género humano. Reunen en sí las cualidades más detestables que deshonran nuestra naturaleza" (I, 83).

Imagine, then, the surprise and indignation of Campoamor when he discovered that the idol of his philosophical enemies, Krause, following the human tendency to imagine a paradise lying somewhere beyond the horizon, affirmed that the Pacific Archipelago was to be the future Eden of mankind, which there alone would find happiness! Campoamor retorted, in his *Polémicas con el panenteísmo,* that such an unrealistic attitude was infinitely more stupid than the eulogies of the Golden Age which Don Quixote uttered while gazing at a handful of acorns (III, 132-33).

Scarcely higher than the Malays, in Campoamor's conception, is the *"casta calmuco-mongola,"* by which he understands the Mongols proper and the Turks—i.e., the southern half of the northern Mongols. He also calls it the *"rama tártaro-mongola,"* and names specifically the Kalmaks, the Kirghiz, and the Cossacks.[9] He brands them as descendants of the Huns and Tartars who, at the order of Ghengis Khan and Tamerlane, subjugated Asia and part of Europe. The devotee of intelligence condemns them as barbarians whose minds are dominated by the concept of force (I, 82).

Campoamor has something approaching respect for the *"casta china,"* of which he says:

"Es la más apreciable y la más ilustrada de cuantas ramas descienden del tronco amarillo" (I, 84).

---

[8] *Vide* Anatole Leroy-Bealieu, *The Empire of the Tsars and the Russians* (New York: Putnam's, 1893), I, 63ff.

[9] Campoamor was wrong in classifying the Cossacks as a race. *Vide* W. P. Cresson, *The Cossacks* (New York: Brentano's, 1919). Campoamor should not be blamed. As Cresson says, "No problem of Russian history has given rise to more controversy than that of the origin of the Cossack race" (p. 5).

In this "caste," he includes the eastern and southern Mongols, the Siamese, Burmese, Talaings ("*peguanos*"), Cochin-Chinese, Annamese ("*tonquineses*"), Chinese, Coreans, Japanese, Tartaro-Chinese, Tibetans, and "*mongües*." Who the "*mongües*" are, I cannot say. Campoamor gives a tolerably accurate picture of the Chinese, but does not differentiate the Japanese from them and envelops the whole "caste" in an accusation of cowardice:

"Su cordura les hace cobardes y su docilidad se convierte en servilismo" (I, 85).

This description could certainly not be applied to the Japanese as we know them. Campoamor did not for a moment foresee that Japan would rise to be a powerful nation:[10]

"Todos los pueblos ribareños de los dos mares contrapuestos de Asia, linfáticos y poltrones, siempre tendrán encorvada la cerviz" (I, 107).

Since Campoamor prized intelligence and despised the Asiatic cult of brute force, it is doubtful if he modified his racial hierarchy in subsequent decades, as he witnessed the rise of Japan to imperial fame. He probably felt that the "yellow peril" denounced in Europe was quite real and much more imminent than the "yellow peril" of contagious stagnation which had alarmed him in earlier years.

---

[10]It was in 1853—i.e., two years before *El personalismo* appeared—that the United States sent Commodore Perry to Japan, but it was only the Russo-Japanese War (1904), three years after the death of Campoamor, which convinced Westerners that Nippon would not accept its fate as had the rest of the Orient. *Vide* David Murray, *Japan* (in "The Story of the Nations"; New York: Putnam's, 1906). The favorite book on Japan at the time was R. Hildreth, *Japan as it was and is* (1855, 56, and 61; revised edition, Chicago: McClurg, 1906). *Vide* also, Joseph H. Longford, *The Story of Old Japan* (New York: Longmans Green, 1910), Okakura-Kakuzo, *The Awakening of Japan* (New York: Japan society, 1921), J. Ingram Bryan, *The Civilization of Japan* (in "Home University Library"; New York: Henry Holt, 1928).

CHAPTER X

THE WHITE RACE—THE ARAB-INDIAN BRANCH

CAMPOAMOR establishes for the white race a permanent presidency over the rest of humanity. His basic racial belief is thus formulated in *El personalismo:*

"La raza blanca es superior a todas las demás, así en fuerzas físicas como en vigor intelectual" (I, 86).

This superiority is shared by both of the halves into which Campoamor divides the white race: namely, the Arab-Indian and the Caucasian. Of these two, the Caucasian is placed higher. Indeed, Campoamor's praise of the Arab-Indian branch is in a minor key and does not convey any enthusiasm. The Arabs and the Hindus cannot boast of nitid skins and are consequently not at the top of the chromatic scale. Moreover, they are geographically situated nearer to the infamous and to the mediocre Orientals. Beside the color scale, Campoamor seems to recognize a rough geographic hierarchy, beginning with central Africa, circumscribing the world in an east to west direction, and reaching full-circle in western Europe, i.e. England and France. A move toward the Orient, on this scale, usually represents a decline.

The moral justification for Campoamor's racial hierarchy is the idea of responsibility. The superior peoples, above all the English, behave, he tells us, in a responsible manner and display moderation, reflection, tenacity without fanaticism, steadiness and steadfastness. Campoamor directs against the Arab-Indians a reproach to which, in a lesser degree, he subjects the Mediterranean Caucasians: namely, that they lack poise and go from one extreme to another:

"La rama árabe-indiana es tan exagerada en su escepticismo como en sus creencias, tan extremada en su postración como en su entusiasmo. De este tronco han salido todos los grandes fundadores de sistemas religiosos, Moisés y Mahoma, que eran casi compatriotas. Asimismo descendían de este tronco los fundadores de las grandes monarquías del Oriente, tan rápidamente fundadas como ruidosa e instantáneamente destruidas. A vueltas de este ardor guerrero y religioso, esta casta siempre ha adolecido de una profunda desidia. Al lado de este alarmante principio: 'La espada es la llave del cielo,' profesa esta resignación estúpida: 'Estaba escrito' " (I, 86).

As for the Arabs, they incline rather toward bellicose intolerance:

"Los árabes no dejan nunca de propender al fanatismo y a la tiranía" (I, 72).

Campoamor scorned them as belonging to the eastern, inferior half of the white race, but he had no hatred for them as the traditional enemies of Christianity. Campoamor's philosophic animus was aimed rather at the imperialism of Catholic Rome:

> "El hierro que en manos de Saladino[1] defendía la independencia y la benignidad, en manos de muchos príncipes cristianos defendió la crueldad y la opresión" (I, 137).

This does not mean that Campoamor had any love or respect for Islam. Like Voltaire, he hated its intolerance; he cites with disgust Caliph Omar's biblioclasm at Alexandria in the seventh century.[2] He had, moreover, an anti-clerical's dislike for a system of government in which the temporal and the spiritual powers were limited. Yet, although Campoamor was not Catholic enough to hate the enemies of the Faith, he was sufficiently patriotic to dislike the hereditary foes of his country. He points out a fact which is seldom recognized: that the Arabs still regard Spain as *terra irredenta:*

> "Los árabes, inflamados todavía por sus ardientes tradiciones, aun deliran con volver a España, más que a reconquistar un país que poseyeron sus mayores por espacio de setecientos ochenta años, a ver a sus imanes rendir preces desde la Giralda de Sevilla" (I, 228).

It is therefore not surprising that Campoamor greeted the Tetuán expedition[3] with a *romance* in the traditional style. The closing lines reveal how the Spaniard felt that the blot inflicted on Spain's escutcheon at Guadalete was at long last avenged:

> "Y al partir, para barrer
> ese inmenso lupanar,
> O'Donnell ríe, Prim vota,
> llora y jura Satanás;
> y esto en sueños dice Ros
> que habló con don Sebastián:
> —¡Valor! ¡y a Alcázar-Quivir[4]

---

[1] *Vide* Charles J. Rosebault, *Saladin, Prince of Chivalry* (New York: McBride, 1930).

[2] *Vide* Stanley Lane-Poole, *A History of Egypt. Vol. VI The Middle Ages* (New York: Scribner's, 1901), 12. Lane-Poole proves that the burning of the library at Alexandria is a legend.

[3] *Vide* Emeterio S. Santovenia, *Prim, el caudillo estadista* (in "Vidas españolas e hispanoamericanas del siglo xix"; Madrid: Espasa-Calpe, 1933), chap. vi, "La guerra de Africa."

[4] Sebastian, King of Portugal (1554-1578) was killed by the Moors at the disastrous battle of Alcazarquivir.

y a Guadalete vengad!
—¡Salve oh rey! ¡Guad-el-Jelú
su Guadalete será!
—¿Nos veremos?—Nos veremos.—
¿Cuándo?—El seis—¿Dónde?—En Tetuán" (IV, 226).

Toward the Jews, Campoamor was much more kindly disposed. He had none of the Spanish hatred for the murderers of Christ. He has penned, in *El personalismo*, a brief but decidedly favorable picture of the Jewish religion, beginning thus:

"El judaísmo, como todos los deísmos, es una religión que sólo puede acomodar a una casta tan inteligente como la israelita" (I, 267).

In enumerating the "intelligent, energetic, personal, and superior peoples" who have been skeptical toward speculative philosophy, Campoamor first names the Jews (I, 354). This would seem to contradict his blaming Spinoza for having set the nebulous ball of German philosophy rolling; it is true that he never thinks of Spinoza as a Jew. Campoamor, the exponent of tolerance, feels above all pity for a race which has borne its long exile with such desperate pride (I, 72-73). He censures the persecution of Jews and cites, as an infamous example, the massacres committed by Christian Crusaders on their way to redeem the Holy Sepulcher (I, 225).[5] Campoamor's dislike for the Crusades is patent.

In brief, Campoamor's attitude was approximately that of Unamuno: he disliked the Arabs but admired the Jews. Admittedly, in neither respect were his feelings as strong as those of Unamuno. Pardo-Bazán hated both the Arabs and the Jews; an attitude which has been much more prevalent in Catholic Spain.

---

[5] *Vide* H. Hagenmeyer, *Chronologie de la première croisade* (Paris: Leroux, 1902). Hagenmeyer quotes a large number of documents describing the persecution of Jews by the Crusaders.

CHAPTER XI

THE WHITE RACE. CAUCASIAN BRANCH. SOUTHERN GROUP

CAMPOAMOR subdivides the western half of the white race, in its turn, into a southern and a northern half. This basic principle is thus formulated in *El personalismo*:

"La rama caucasiana, originaria del tronco blanco, se subdivide en *meridional* y *septentrional*. A la primera pertenecen todos los pueblos europeos que baña el Mediterráneo" (I, 86-87).

The definition of the *"rama meridional"* is not quite satisfactory in that it does not comprise Portugal or Rumania, while it includes the South Slavs of the Adriatic. The division of the two groups is not consistent in that Campoamor eulogizes France, which is a member of the southern, or inferior group. This can be explained only by adopting the usual division of France into a southern and a northern half, *pays d'oc* and *pays d'oïl*, as it were. Germany, which theoretically belongs to the northern group, is condemned as a fanatical, orientalized country. Does Campoamor admit that his predestined races can be influenced by outside influences? Is his geographical distinction meant to be merely a convenient description of the present location of these peoples, or is it an implicit admission that races are modified by climate? In any case, it is ironical that the exponents of the race-theory should thus be as it were maliciously deprived of the fruits of their philosophy.

Campoamor does not hesitate to stress the inferiority of the southern group of the Caucasian branch of the white race, although this involves ranking the Spanish people in the second class. He accuses the southern group of displaying an almost oriental lack of moderation:

"Aunque no tan extremados como los blancos de Asia, los europeos meridionales exageran extraordinariamente todos sus sentimientos y todas sus ideas" (I, 87).

He later declares, in a half-disgusted, half-despairing vein, that the Mediterranean races are forever condemned to this ridiculous rôle:

"Las naciones galo-célticas, que hoy ocupan el antiguo mundo romano, constantemente arrastrarán su *medianía*, ora con gloria, ora con vituperio. Parlachines y vanidosos, nunca los importará representar el papel de primeras víctimas, con tal que se persuadan de que representan el primer papel" (I, 107).

The first logical consequence of this condemnation of the Mediterranean is a dislike of classical antiquity. Campoamor did not hesitate to express his impatience to shake off what he considered to be the stupid cult of classicism:

"Divorciémonos de la antigüedad que se ha vuelto loca" (I, 23).

In his hatred of Antiquity lies one of Campoamor's chief differences from Voltaire. There is here, no doubt, an echo of the quarrel between the Ancients and the Moderns. Campoamor's principal criticism of the ancient world was that it lacked a philosophical background and that its history was invariably inspired by petty or low motives. In his reactionary period, Campoamor succeeded in whipping up a respectable respect for Antiquity. In *Lo absoluto*, he went so far as to accuse Descartes of gross plagiarizing of Plato (I, 548-49). However, his admiration was accorded only to "pre-Christian" writers such as Plato. For the rest of Antiquity, he maintained his previous scorn.

His "Christianity" gave him an excuse for condemning classical mythology more harshly than ever, branding it as fundamentally false. He had never been favorably disposed toward the ancient deities. In *El personalismo*, he had quarreled with the neo-paganism of Goethe and arraigned Jupiter, Apollo, Diana, and Venus, whom he regarded as monsters of iniquity (I, 266).

On account of his dislike for the mentality of the ancient world, Campoamor could not feel the appeal of its plastic arts. Even in his reactionary period, he refused to pay homage to the revered masterpieces they had produced. In his *Poética*, he says scornfully:

"Si la Venus de Milo con su cabeza de chorlito pudiese ser animada por un nuevo Pigmaleón, sería la verdadera imagen del arte sin filosofía, una mujer muy hermosa, pero enteramente estúpida" (III, 310).

This is admittedly true of decadent classical art, but it may be affirmed that, in denying completely the existence of any philosophical background in Antiquity, Campoamor was really confessing his own blindness. Unamuno displayed more comprehension in this respect.

Ancient Rome has been condemned by many Spanish writers, notably Unamuno. However, it would seem irreverent to subject Greece to excessive criticism. Yet Campoamor does not hesitate to dismiss Greek history as one long manifestation of meridional exaggeration:

"Los pequeños estados de Grecia, convirtiendo en nacional una afrenta doméstica, se confederaron para lanzarse en masa a la conquista de Troya; después la exaltación de su ardor guerrero impulsó a sus repúblicas a hacer frente, no sin gloria inmarescible, a los interminables ejércitos de los persas; y por último, llevando su rivalidad a la desesperación, estos famosos pueblos acabaron por destruírse recíprocamente, empleando su valor en destrozarse las entrañas" (I, 87).

These lines occur in *El personalismo*. Campoamor expressed the same idea later, in *El ideísmo*, and with much more irony and scorn: he says that all the dissensions and wars of Greece were motivated by petty rivalries, like the cudgel-fights in which the peasants of Asturias indulge, to the shouts of "¡*Viva Pravia!*" and "¡*Muera Piloña!*" (III, 507).

The same scorn for Attica occasionally finds expression in Campoamor's poetry. In the epic *Colón* (1853), Faith, Hope, and Charity, in their "Juicio del Mundo," manifest extreme disdain for Greece:

"Atenas, la que a Aspasias ha admirado,
quédaos ahí con vuestra falsa gloria" (IV, 545).

Campoamor censured Rome with equal severity. In *El personalismo*, he affirms that the anarchy within the walls of Rome was scarcely more tolerable than the despotism which reigned throughout the far-flung empire (I, 87). In his latter years, Campoamor remained equally hostile to Rome. He tells us quite unequivocally in *El ideísmo*:

"A la Roma antigua se la admira, pero no se la ama. Yo ni la admiro ni la amo" (III, 509).

He proceeds to describe Rome as devoid of ideals, avaricious, tyrannical, and domineering:

"La ausencia de toda ideología de la sociedad romana hizo que fuese su Dios el dinero, su derecho la fuerza, su moral la dominación, su administración la rapiña, su política el gobierno de los patricios contra los plebeyos y el fin de todo la esclavitud dentro y la sumisión fuera" (III, 510).

Aristocratic Don Ramón hated above all the republic of virtuous Cato and his peers. He maintained that the emperors, even Nero, were much more human, and blamed Tacitus for having painted a too sombre picture of them and their deeds.[1]

Campoamor's unremitting hatred of republican Rome brought him into sharp conflict with one of the high-priests of Spanish republicanism, Castlelar, who proclaimed that Rome was a paragon for the present day:

---

[1] *Vide* P. Hochart, *Études au sujet de la persécution des Chrétiens sous Néron* (Paris: Leroux, 1885). This is a critical study of Book XV of the *Annals* of Tacitus.

"La historia romana es de grande enseñanza para nuestro siglo y nuestra sociedad. Las luchas que agitaban a la reina de las naciones son nuestras luchas, sus dolores son nuestros dolores, y hasta sus remedios son, por desgracia, también nuestros remedios" (II, 447). Campoamor retorted that Roman history was similar to that loathsome episode, the French Revolution. He proceeded to draw a detailed comparison between the two. The moral he derived from this parallel is:

"Siempre lo mismo. El despotismo vive parced en medio de la anarquía."

Campoamor apparently never mastered Greek, and had a poor knowledge of Greek literature. He received as a boy so thorough a grounding in Latin that he hated the subject for the rest of his life. His clumsy pedagogue was a certain Don Benito, whose methods were almost inquisitorial. In *El personalismo*, his ex-pupil refers to Latin in terms which show that the matter still rankled:

"Es un idioma sin delicadeza, encopetado, sensual y hasta pobre cuando se le sube a las regiones de la inteligencia y de la moral. Aunque espante la evocada sombra de don Benito, concluiré diciendo que de mucha parte del modo de pensar áspero, torpe y material de la sociedad romana, lo mismo de la republicana que de la cesárea, tiene la culpa la lengua latina. ¡Perdón, padre Horacio!" (I, 270). Unamuno would undoubtedly have expressed strong approval of these remarks.

For Christian Rome, Campoamor had even less sympathy. While his Neo-Catholic enemies strove to exalt the Eternal City and the Papacy, our deist referred to both in terms of the utmost contempt. He blamed them for having converted the sweetest, most humanitarian, and most spiritual of religions into a cult as fierce, as intolerant, and almost as fatalistic as Islam. Campoamor reveals his anti-traditionalism by accusing the Spanish Hapsburgs of helping the Papacy in this infernal task (I, 87).

The gravest crime of Catholic Rome has been, according to Campoamor, its relentless imperialism. He takes, as we have said, particular delight in ridiculing the Crusades, which were prepared in such a spirit of ignorance that many of the leaders thought, like Calderón, that Jerusalem was a sea-port. It is significant that this satire occurs in the reactionary work *El ideísmo* (III, 513).

Toward the popes of the Renascence, Campoamor entertained a strong personal dislike. He depicts Alexander VI as a monster of vice and recalls that Isabel the Catholic ordered Gonzalo de Córdoba to convey to him her disapproval of his conduct, which overshadowed the monstrosities of his predecessors (I, 243).[2] Campoamor depicts Julius II as an utterly wordly pope and recalls his significant gesture of throwing keys representing those of Saint Peter into the Tiber and exclaiming that, since the keys of Saint Peter were of no avail to him, he intended to have resort to the sword of Saint Paul (I, 240). In order to illustrate the character of Gregory XIII, Campoamor recalls that this pope expressed approval of the Massacre of Saint Bartholomew, organized public rejoicings for the event, and had it painted in the Vatican as one of the triumphs of the Catholic religion (I, 225).[3]

In the same work which contains these indictments of Renascence popes, *El personalismo*, Campoamor shows admirable equity by painting a touching picture of Pius IX, whose character he reveals in a dramatic anecdote. The Pope, riding through the suburbs of Rome in his carriage saw a crowd gathered around an old man who had fainted and lay stretched out on the ground. The mob shouted scornfully that it was a Jew. The Pope replied that it was a man who was suffering and who needed help. He had the Jew put into his carriage and transported to his house. "*Lo mismo hubiera hecho Jesucristo*," comments Campoamor, apparently forgetting that Christ was a Jew (I, 226). It would be more to the point to say that Pius IX was returning to the traditional benevolence of the Popes toward the Jews, a tradition broken by Leo XII, who had shown great severity in his treatment of them.[4]

It is not surprising, then, that in his traditionalist period Campoamor, forgetting his tirades against Roman imperialism, defended the temporal power of the Pope against those who were seeking to destroy it. In *Lo absoluto*, he affirms that:

"Para corromper los corazones, no hay más que falsear los entendimientos; y todos los Césares tienden a combatir al Papa-Rey para convertir en Papas a los Reyes."

[2] *Vide* William H. Prescott, *History of the Reign of Ferdinand and Isabella the Catholic* (Boston: Phillips Sampson, 1857), II, 333-34.

[3] *Vide* Artaud de Montor, *Histoire des souverains pontifes romains* (Paris: Didot, 1847), IV, 348ff. Montor maintains that Gregory XIII was not responsible, but the people of Rome, who regarded the massacre as a just punishment for the sack of Rome, which had taken place forty-five years earlier. The picture mentioned by Campoamor is attributed to Vasari, although this is denied by Adolfo Venturi, *Storia dell'arte italiana* (Milan: Hoepli, 1933), IX, Part VI, 372.

[4] *Vide* Fredrik Nielsen, *The History of the Papacy in the XIXth Century* (London: John Murray, 1906), II, 24. Campoamor's enemy, Jaime Balmes, wrote a panegyric of Pius IX entitled *Pío IX* (Madrid: Eusebio Aguado, 1847).

He concludes with a dark warning:

"Pero ya recibirán el pago de su ignorancia y de su orgullo esos protestantismos, frutos de la ambición de los reyes y de la corrupción de los pueblos, pero frutos de perdición que llevan entrañada en sí la maldición de la posteridad" (I, 664).

Having taken sides in this then-burning question, Campoamor found himself involved in the polemical literature which was a by-product of the controversy. In *Polémicas con la democracia* (II, 612ff.), he defended the temporal power of the Pope against the writer of an anonymous French pamphlet entitled *Le Pape et le Congrès*. Campoamor would not have taken seriously the paradoxes propounded in this pamphlet, but for the wide success with which they met.[5] To Campoamor's dismay, Escosura reproduced these ideas in a booklet called *España, Napoleón,*

---

[5] The pamphlet (1859) was commonly attributed to the Vicomte de la Guéronnière (1816-1875), a pamphleteer who was regarded as the mouthpiece of Napoleon III. The opuscule *Le Pape et le Congrès* was translated into Spanish and published under the title *El Papa i el Congreso* (Bogotá, 1860). The French original provoked an international controversy. Some fifty or more replies were published, the most noteworthy being (all are dated 1860):

C. L. de Camusat de Riancey, *Le patriotisme et la foi, en réponse à l'auteur* . . . . *de l'écrit Le Pape et le Congrès. Un mot aux quarante-cinq brochures. Par un Catholique.*

Count Desbassayns de Richemont, *Un mot d'un laique sur la brochure Le Pape et le Congrès.*

F. A. P. Dupanloup [Bishop of Orleans], *La brochure Le Pape et le Congrès.* This in its turn provoked a number of replies, notably:

    L'Evêque d'Orleans et la brochure Le Pape et le Congrès. Par un vrai Catholique

    J. Choutard, *Guelfes et Gibelins. Lettre à propos de la brochure de l'Evêque d'Orléans*

    A. P. Grandguillot, *Lettre d'un Journaliste Catholique, à l'Evêque d'Orléans*

    P. Redins, *Le Pape et son pouvoir temporel, réflexions sur les deux publications* . . . . .

O. P. Gerbet [Bishop of Perpignan], *De la Papauté, en réponse à l'écrit, intitulé Le Pape et le Congrès.*

A. F. Nettement, *Appel au bon sens, au droit, et à l'histoire, en réponse à la brochure Le Pape et le Congrès.*

M. Orsini, *Réponse à la brochure intitulée: "Le Pape et le Congrès."*

P. L. Parisis, *L'Evêque d'Arras à l'auteur de la brochure Le Pape et le Congrès.*

C. H. A. Plantier, [Bishop of Nîmes] *De la brochure intitulée: "Le Pape et le Congrès."*

J. J. F. Poujoulat, *Les droits du pape.* . . .

Count C. Solaro della Margherita, *Réponse à l'opuscule "Le Pape et le Congrès."*

Prince A. Trubetskoi, *Réflexions sur la brochure Le Pape et le Congrès.*

Viscount de Grondy, *De la question romaine et de la politique actuelle* (Saint Gall, 1860) (contains a "Paraphrase critique de la brochure: 'Le Pape et le Congrès' ").

Roma (1860).[6] Our traditionalist's ineffective reply was an assertion that Escosura must be joking.

He hated the House of Savoy as the enemy of the Papacy. To this feeling was added disgust caused by Victor Emanuel's cession of Nice and Savoy:

> "Victor Manuel, el descendiente de la casa de Saboya, la más antigua de las casas reinantes, trueca el ducado que ha sido cuna y tumba de casi todos sus mayores por ceñirse la corona de hierro de los lombardos" (II, 619).[7]

We have already described how Campoamor's attitude toward Gothic architecture changed from one of indifference to one of reverence. A parallel development was a growing antipathy toward the Italian Renascence. There is in *El ideísmo* a sarcastic description of the art of Michael Angelo, whose relationship with the papacy Campoamor fails completely to mention:

> "Miguel Angel, que al llegar a viejo se hizo un gruñón, llamaba "bárbaro" al arte gótico. Y es que este genio de la escultura, de la pintura y de la arquitectura era un verdadero godo que no comprendía la filosofía del arte [??], que es *su aplicación a su natural objeto.* Cuando satisfecho de su Moisés, que es un hércules que da miedo, le dijo ¡Parla!, la estatua debió de romper a hablar para rogarle que le modificase aquellos cuernecitos, que sólo una enorme buena voluntad puede suponer que son rayos de luz y que le dan la apariencia de un Satanás de comedia y que además le arreglase un poco aquellas barbas mayores que las del río Betis de Herrera. En su pintura de la creación del hombre, parece que Dios, arrepentido de su hechura, le señala, delatándole a la policía de sus angelitos, para que le lleven a la cárcel" (III, 492-93).

The criticism of the statue of Moses[8] reveals that Campoamor did not know that Michael Angelo was following a medieval—and consequently a Gothic!—tradition, while the comments on the painting of the "Crea-

---

[6] This pamphlet of Patricio de la Escosura (1807-1878) had considerable success, at least two editions being published. This politician and writer was passing through a difficult period of his life. He had taken part in riots against O'Donnell, and, presenting himself as a candidate for the *partido progresista* and an enemy of the *Unión Liberal,* had failed to obtain a seat in the elections of 1858.

[7] *Vide* W. J. Stillman, *The Union of Italy* (Cambridge University Press, 1909), 307ff.

[8] *Vide* John Addington Symonds, *The Life of Michelangelo Buonarroti* (3rd edit.; London, Macmillan, 1901), II, 83ff.

tion of Man" show a lamentable insensitiveness to grandeur and mystery.[9]

Campoamor's vulgar attack on Michael Angelo seems all the more heinous in view of the enthusiastic applause which he accorded to the ephemeral art of his day. In *El personalismo*, he expresses fervent admiration for Rossini (admittedly an idol of last-century music lovers[10]), and classes him with Archimedes, Thucidides, Herodotus, Galileo and Pascal (I, 237). In *Lo absoluto*, he describes Canova's statue of Venus[11] and Verdi's opera *Il Trovatore*[12] as two of the outstanding works of art which humanity has produced (I, 676). Reactionary Campoamor blames Michael Angelo for having destroyed the Christian art of the Middle Ages (which incidentally is untrue), but he fails to see that there is nothing Christian about the works of Canova or Verdi.

Campoamor's attitude toward Italian politics and art was, therefore, mixed and rather inconsistent. He was truly Spanish in that he always despised the Italian people, regarding them as the dregs of Europe. Speaking of slanderous articles appearing in Spain about the exiled Queen Cristina, he says:

> "Al leer lo que han escrito de ella algunos periodistas de una sapiencia y de una moralidad anónimas, debe avergonzarse de que existan semejantes españoles, aun después de haberse criado entre italianos" (I, 336-37).

Campoamor obviously fails to rise above the level of the calumny he is rebuking. In any case, Italy is theoretically only one rung lower than Spain in the hierarchy of races established by Campoamor.

Here, following his scale, is the place to analyze his interpretation of Spain. It seems, however, preferable to discuss first the whole of the outside world and then to show the Spain of Campoamor against this background.

---

[9] *Vide* Charles Hobroyd, *Michael Angelo Buonarroti* (London: Duckworth, 1903), chap. vi.

[10] A typical expression of this admiration is A. Pougin, *Rossini: notes, impressions, souvenirs, commentaires* (Paris, 1870).

[11] Presumably the "Venere uscente dal bagno," in the Uffizi Gallery in Florence.

[12] On the renown of Verdi, *vide* Frederick J. Crowest, *Verdi: Man and Musician* (London: Milne, 1897), 223ff.

CHAPTER XII

FRANCE

FRANCE deserves to be studied separately, not only on account of the important rôle it plays in Campoamor's ideology, but also because of his incertitude as to whether he should classify it with the Mediterranean or with the nordic nations.

Thinking no doubt of Napoleon I and also Napoleon III, he says, in *El personalismo*, that the main defect of this great nation is Cæsarism:

"La nación galo-franca, a pesar de estar constituída en su mayoría por una raza de organización notable, participa de todos los defectos inherentes a las cualidades de que carece. Con su excesiva vanidad, se exalta hasta el más alto punto de emulación a la voz de quien la gobierna y, con su gran instinto imitativo, parodia las grandezas y las pequeñeces del que la sabe mandar" (I, 142).

In this respect, it is important to remember that *El personalismo* appeared in 1855.

Despite these reproaches, Campoamor was full of benevolence toward France. In "El tren expreso" (one of *Los pequeños poemas*, although ironically it is twenty pages long), he relates a chance meeting with a French lady in a train. Here is a significant remark:

"Podéis—la repliqué con arrogancia—
la hermosura alabar de vuestro suelo,
pues creo, como hay Dios, que es vuestra Francia
un país tan hermoso como el cielo" (VIII, 23).

This gallantry is admittedly commonplace, but it nevertheless represents Campoamor's attitude.

However, the Spaniard found in France not only a pleasant country, but above all an intellectual tradition to which, as a youth, he, the future skeptic, became attached because of the very vetoes of intolerant ecclesiastics. As he relates in *El personalismo:*

"La principal razón que he tenido para leer los filósofos franceses es la de que estaban *prohibidos;* las diatribas lanzadas contra ellos desde el púlpito por sacerdotes indiscretos son los reclamos que me han conducido a la enramada donde se oculta la serpiente tentadora. . . . Así pues, a pesar y con motivo de ser libros *prohibidos,* la filosofía francesa fué, durante un largo período de mi juventud, mi exclusivo pasto espiritual" (I, 284-86).

In view of this experience, it is not surprising that Campoamor constantly idealizes French philosophy as the liberator of the human mind from the tyranny of the mediæval Church. It shares this honor, in his opinion, with Martin Luther, whom, as we shall see, Campoamor converts from a Protestant devil into a nordic hero:

"El empirismo francés .... parece un joven que, aburrido, desesperado por las exigencias, celos y extravagancias de la infecunda vieja Sorbona, se lanza con furor en el camino de todas las emancipaciones humanas, renegando de esta octogenaria y de toda su innumerable parentela" (I, 285).

Descartes was one of the great obsessions of Campoamor. The poet's references to the French philosopher are usually immoderate. At first sight they seem hopelessly contradictory. It is, however, possible to trace a definite development in the Spaniard's attitude. In his liberal period, he idealized Descartes as the founder of French skepticism. He says in *El personalismo:*

"La filosofía *moderna* o *psicológica* empieza en Descartes. Este Cervantes de la caballería escolástica acabó con todas las follones y malandrines de la Edad media" (I, 289).

The other side of the picture was for him Descartes' rôle as the inspirer of German philosophy, which, as we have already explained, the Spaniard regarded as a useless rigmarole.

In his reactionary period, our ex-liberal branded Descartes as a radical, a perverter of society. In his *discurso de entrada* at the Academy, he revealed this change of attitude by berating Descartes for plagiarizing the Spaniard Gómez Pereira in his dictum, *"Je pense, donc je suis"* (I, 410).[1] In *Lo absoluto*, he comes out openly against the dangerous radical and affirms that:

"El cartesianismo, además de ser un materialismo vergonzante, es un escepticismo desvergonzado" (I, 537).

The quips with which the liberal had satirized German philosophy are mild in comparison with the crude insults with which the reactionary describes Descartes, who, he says, speaks with *"una jactancia más inconsciente que la de un apilador de yeso"* (I, 539). In *El ideísmo*, he replies to P. Ceferino González, who had accused him of pantheism, that theologians should realize that the real danger comes from Cartesian

---

[1]The relationship between Gómez Pereira and Descartes has been the subject of an extensive literature. *Vide* Marcelino Menéndez y Pelayo, "La 'Antoniana Margarita' de Gómez Periera," *La ciencia española* (Madrid: Victoriano Suárez, 1933), I, 465ff.

skepticism, which has led mankind to the present *"estado patológico que es el* delirium tremens *de todo orgullo y de toda rebelión"* (III, 465). In a way, our turn-coat was throwing out this anti-Cartesianism as a smoke-screen with which to cover up his own heterodoxy.

The poet has given verse form to these ideas in the *dolora* "La fe y la razón," in which he attacks Descartes through the mouth of the Queen of Sweden:

> "¡O maldito escepticismo!
> ¿No estáis viendo, hombre inhumano,
> que con atroz ateísmo
> lanza vuestra impía mano
> a Dios y al mundo a un abismo,
> siendo el pensamiento humano
> de sus juicios soberano
> y único juez de sí mismo?" (V, 155).

Descartes expresses pained surprise at the accusation of Christina. Campoamor concludes:

> "Cuando Descartes murió,
> Cristina del *sé que sé*
> las consecuencias sacó
> y a Monaldeschi mató
> dió a su trono un puntapié
> su religión abjuró
> y al fin refugio buscó
> en la católica fe . . .
> el célebre *sé que sé*
> dió al olvido—y, de este modo,
> halló la ciencia en la fe
> ultima verdad del todo" (V, 157).[2]

That Campoamor should attribute to Descartes any remark such as *"sé que sé"* shows how completely the reactionary had lost all sense of equity. We are more impressed by the dignified periods of Pascal:

> "C'est le coeur que sent Dieu, et non la raison. Voilà ce que c'est que la foi, Dieu sensible au coeur, non à la raison."

It is surprising that the Spaniard did not imitate this noble tone, for he knew and venerated Pascal, especially in his early Catholic and late reactionary periods. To Pascal he has devoted the *dolora* "El sexto

---

[2] *Vide* I. A. Taylor, *Christina of Sweden* (London: Hutchinson, 1909).

sentido," writing as though he were describing a Heaven-sent peer of Christ. God announces:

"Quiero hacer al mundo dón
de un hombre de alma gigante,
grande cual la religión,
como la gloria brillante.

Fe y saber broten de sus labios
cual brota el verano flores,
más docto que los más sabios
más bueno que los mejores.

De la humana criatura
cese el eclipse moral.
¡Salve a mi mejor hechura!
Dijo, y nació Blas Pascal" (V, 174).

To the more orthodox fellow-Catholics of Pascal, Malebranche and Bossuet, Campoamor became attached in his reactionary period. He made respectful reference to both in his *Discurso* at the Academy (I, 387-88). This represented an implicit recantation of his earlier ideas, since Bossuet embodies both theology and the philosophy of history, which he had despised.

However, Campoamor was much more interested in the French philosophy of the eighteenth than of the seventeenth century. In particular, Montesquieu was his guide and master. Campoamor relates, in *El personalismo* (I, 380), how under this influence, he wrote his *Filosofía de las leyes*; how lawyers resented this intrusion into their domain; how their reproof was neutralized by praise from others, including "the well-known writer" Monlau in his *Higiene pública*[3]; how Campoamor accepted the applause rather than the blame and incorporated a considerable amount of the early work in *El personalismo*. In order to describe the early Campoamor, then, it would be necessary to invent from Montesquieu an adjective similar to "Voltairian." Alas! Not even to this his master was Campoamor faithful during his reactionary period. In *Lo absoluto*, he berates "*vosotros, codificadores oficiales, raza materialista, hija legítima de Montesquieu el empírico*" (I, 642).

Campoamor clearly owes a great deal to Voltaire, whose ideas he

---

[3]Pedro Felipe Monlau (1808-1871), a polymath and, above all, a doctor. His *Elementos de higiene pública* appeared in 1847 (2nd edit., 1862).

frequently quotes. Although the two have much in common, Campoamor affirms, in *El personalismo* (I, 286), his dislike of the negative spirit of Voltaire. The Spaniard is certainly difficult to please; he criticizes German philosophy for having erected systems and condemns Voltaire for having failed to do so. Admittedly, lack of system reduces Voltaire's thoughts to *"un chaos d'idées claires,"* whereas Montesquieu attempts to be consistent.

Rousseau's fate was similar to that of Montesquieu. Although many things separated them, particularly the question of communism, Campoamor in his liberal period proclaimed his deep admiration for Jean-Jacques, whose combination of anti-traditionalist philosophy and poetic temperament was no doubt attractive to the Spaniard. He affirms, in *El personalismo*, that:

> "El empirismo francés, cuya representación más genuina y más concreta es Rousseau, oso desde las cejas abajo, y desde las cejas arriba Pericles, es un materialismo ateniense" (I, 285).

The change in Campoamor's attitude is evident in the notorious *Discurso*, where he refers to:

> "El filosofastro . . . . Rousseau, el creador de tantas Julias de carne y hueso que convierten el vicio en una sublimidad" (I, 389).

In the same spirit, he says in *Lo absoluto:*

> "No hagáis caso de Rousseau, de ese apologizador del hombre bestia" (I, 628).

Indeed, Campoamor evidently hopes, in the *Discurso*, to curry favor with the reactionaries of the Academy by recanting and denouncing all French thought of the eighteenth century, which he describes as *filosofismo*, expounded by *filosofistas*, as opposed to *filosofía* and *filósofos*. The word *filosofismo* recalls Unamuno's *cientifismo*. Campoamor asks indignantly:

> "¿Quiénes han inundado el mundo de lágrimas y sangre más que esos lógicos de ideas incompletas, esos filosofistas de la Enciclopedia, que, tomando una quimera o una paradoja por un sistema, han desterrado la delicadeza de la sociedad, la virtud de la moral y a Dios de la teodicea, convirtiendo al padre de familia en una autoridad usurpadora [rubbish!], al sacerdote en un mueble inútil y al magistrado en un verdugo![!?]" (I, 394-95).

In *Lo absoluto*, Campoamor waxes particularly indignant against Condorcet, and more especially against his report on the learned societies of Europe, in which he counseled the Spanish authorities to pay no attention to the religious beliefs of candidates (I, 440-41).[4]

One result of the French philosophy of the eighteenth century was the French Revolution, regarding which Campoamor's attitude suffered something of the usual change. During his liberal period, he applauded the dethronement of the Catholic Church. After depicting the futility of scholastic debates in *El personalismo*, he concludes:

"¡Quién creerá que nuestros dichosos frailes han vivido muchos siglos engrescados en esta guerra imaginativa hasta que los sacó, algo bruscamente, es cierto, de esta inteligente ociosidad el látigo de la revolución!" (I, 289).

At the same time, he expresses strong disapproval of the Revolution itself, with all its excesses:

"La gran revolución francesa es un enorme borracho cuyo hediondo aspecto es un vivo y eterno ejemplo de temperancia" (I, 336).

It would be superfluous to explain that, as the years passed, Campoamor became increasingly hostile to the French Revolution.

The hatred of Spaniards toward 1789 is due largely to 1808. There was in nineteenth century Spain a kind of *leyenda negra* of the *francesada*. Like Pardo-Bazán, Campoamor had a vivid atavic memory of the destruction committed by the Napoleonic invaders at Miraflores. To this episode he has devoted an indignant poem entitled "En la cartuja de Burgos." Addressing the invading soldiery, he cries:

"¡Fuego, embriagada tropa!
Talad, brindando por el culto ibero
tinta en licor la ropa
ayer en esa copa
la sangre se libaba del cordero" (IV, 259-60).

Admittedly, this is abominable poetry.

It is not surprising that Campoamor, in his reactionary period, should be an ardent admirer of the excoriater of the Revolution, Chateaubriand. Forgetting that Chateaubriand began as a *philosophe* and became a Catholic conservative only under the stress of events, the Spanish diehard makes the following naïve suggestion in *El ideísmo:*

"Si Chateaubriand hubiera nacido algunos años antes . . . . tal vez

---

[4]Campoamor is confused. He is probably thinking of the "Avis aux Espagnols," *Oeuvres complètes de Condorcet* (Brunswick: Vieweg, 1804), XVI, 315ff., in which Condorcet attributes the decadence of Spain to religious tyranny.

hubiera evitado la revolución francesa, haciendo levantar et bloqueo
que contra la ciudad de su Dios pusieron Voltaire y Rousseau prin-
cipalmente, con sólo dirigir contra ellos las diatribas y los sarcasmos
que desde el otro mundo lanzó contra . . . . Napoleón" (III, 518).

As it was, Chateaubriand's efforts seemed vain, for, when he had
completed his reactionary labor, the whole cycle began once more.
There arose in France a Neo-Cartesian movement led by Bordas-
Demoulin, who published in 1843 his work *Le cartésianisme*.   The
reactionary Campoamor of *Lo absoluto* condemns it as harshly as he
does the original sin of Cartesianism.   He describes it as:

"Este cartesianismo recalentado, que no es más que una mezcla de
un sensualismo desnaturalizado y de un idealismo echado a perder"
(I, 531).

Campoamor was undoubtedly prejudiced by the fact that Bordas-
Demoulin, although a sincere Christian, was a vindex of the Revolution.
In this connection, Campoamor found himself in diplomatic difficul-
ties.   Neo-Cartesianism spread throughout Europe, and found a Spanish
representative in Nicomedes Martín Mateos,[5] who dedicated his book
El espiritualismo (1861) to Campoamor himself.   In reply, the poet
acknowledged this homage with uneasy grace and proceeded to subject
Neo-Cartesianism to harsh criticism (id.).

With the even more radical school of socialists, Campoamor had
mixed relations, even in his liberal youth.   He was deeply influenced
by Saint Simon, whom he frequently quotes.   In particular, he expresses,
in *El personalismo*, his enthusiastic approval of Saint-Simon's remark
that the Golden Age lies before us, and that our children will see it
some day, our own task being to make clear the way (I, 175).   On the
contrary, Fourier is dismissed as a happy madman:

"Fourier . . . . anulando la personalidad, falseando por su base el
objeto de la creación, aspira en sus seráficos ensueños a hacer de la
especie humana una única familia igualmente ilustrada e igualmente
venturosa" (I, 241).

In order to appreciate the irony of these remarks we must recall Campoamor's theories concerning the social hierarchy.
For our anti-socialist liberal, even as he veered toward reaction, the
ideal form of government was most closely approached by the régime

---

[5]Nicomedes Martín Mateos was one of the outstanding Spanish philosophers of the
nineteenth century.   Unfortunately for his relations with Campoamor, he was a liberal:
he quarreled with the reactionary Donoso Cortés.

of Louis Philippe. This question separated him from Castelar, who, after 1848, declared that this upheaval proved that the Spanish Partido Moderado entertained impractical ideas and that only the Partido Democrático could lead to happiness. Campoamor retorted that the natural consequence of democracy was the French Revolution, with all its appalling bloodshed. In order to illustrate this antithesis, to his own advantage naturally, Campoamor has imagined, in *Polémicas con la democracia*, a conversation between Castelar and himself, the one condemning Louis-Philippe, the other the Revolution. It begins thus:

> Castelar: "¿Qué *ideal* se propuso realizar el partido moderado? La monarquía doctrinaria de *Luis Felipe*. La historia ha juzgado ya ese ideal y la cólera de Dios lo ha barrido del mundo."

> Campoamor: "....¡Oh Calégula! ¡Oh Nerón! ¡Oh Tigelino! tiranos grandes y pequeños de los siglos pasados, consolaos en vuestros sepulcros, pues los que debieron ser hijos de la libertad, sobrepujaron vuestros caprichos y furores" (II, 442-43).

Campoamor reaches the insulting conclusion that:

"El señor Castelar no *escribe* la historia, la *hace*" (II, 446).

When Campoamor was at the height of his intellectual power, the Second Empire in France was passing through its early phase of brilliant success. Its example, like the fascism of today, was contagiating the rest of Europe. Campoamor, at the time a liberal, thought that its influence should be strenuously opposed. To this subject he devoted a vigorous speech in the Cortes on July 14, 1857, regarding the proposed reform of the constitution:

> "Hoy la forma de Gobierno más preponderante en el mundo es la que se ha dado en llamar forma de gobierno imperial, hoy el viento de la moda gubernamental viene exclusivamente de París. El Gobierno de S.M., acaso sin caer en ello, sin duda nos quiere trasladar a España una especie de imperialismo, pero sin Emperador" (II, 323).

As he became more dogged in his attempts to push the waters of progress up-stream, Campoamor developed an admiration for Napoleon III as the symbol of law and order:

> "Los moderados decíamos precisamente que era *Napoleón* el *ultra-grande*, cuando las progresistas le llamaban el *pequeño*, pero aunque *Napoleón III* fuese para nosotros tres veces más grande que el

primero, no tiene nada que ver para que le juzguemos sin adularle, y sea siempre para nosotros . . . . el antiguo restaurador del orden europeo" (II, 616).

These lines from *Polémicas con la democracia* reveal Campoamor's doubts as to the consistency of his arguments. If he praised Napoleon III, should not Napoleon I be given credit as the founder of the line and of the system, although it has naturally led to the *francesada?* Indeed, Campoamor feared that Napoleon III might try in Spain the same policy which had won for him Nice and Savoy at the expense of Italy. The Spaniard saw the peril as a reality which only the Emperor's Spanish wife, Eugenia María de Montijo, had averted:

"Si hoy no se sentase en el trono de Francia una española, tan célebre por su hermosura como por sus virtudes, y *Luis Napoleón* no tuviese una rémora que le impidiese revolver sus armas contra nosotros y mandase a Aragón, Vizcaya y Cataluña, de heraldos revolucionarios, unos cuantos *Garibaldis* al pormenor, y después que fomentasen los instintos de independencia provincial, lanzase sobre España un ejército de doscientos mil hombres, creando una república en Tolosa, y la capital de un reino en Zaragoza o Barcelona: en virtud de qué derecho . . . . serían desmembradas esas provincias de la monarquía española?" (II, 617-18).

In other words, Campoamor feared that Napoleon III would revive the plans of Bonaparte for establishing the Ebro as the Franco-Spanish frontier.

The poet-philosopher was influenced by the French writers of the time of Louis-Philippe and Napoleon III almost as much as by the *philosophes* of the preceding century. Even Balzac has left his trace in Campoamor's work, although the poet did not write a single novel and showed no interest in the genus. In the *dolora* "A . . . . ,"[6] Campoamor says:

"No doy los tristes pensamientos míos
por tus sueños, ligeros y rosados;
porque a cráneos vacíos
prefiero corazones disecados."

These verses constitute a reply to the question which Balzac asks at the beginning of *Le Père Goriot:*

---

[6] *Vide* Andrés González Blanco, 110-11. This *dolora* is to be found in *Doloras y poemas* (Paris: Garnier, 1888), 287, but it seems to have been omitted from the *Obras completas.*

"Qui décidera de ce qui est plus horrible à voir, ou des cœurs desséchés, ou des crânes vides?"[7]

The nineteenth-century French writer who exercised the greatest influence on Campoamor was Victor Hugo. This is evident not only in the Spaniard's ideas, but even in his prose-style. Campoamor liked to write a series of paragraphs of one period each, the periods being sententious aphorisms often involving metaphors of the kind which delighted Victor Hugo: Here is an example from *El personalismo:*

"La ignorancia es la orfandad del alma.
La educación es una transfiguración.
Así como la instrucción pone alas a las inteligencias perspicuas, echa quintales de plomo sobre las ambiciones ilegítimas" (I, 172).

It was a commonplace among Spanish admirers of Campoamor to affirm that he was "greater" than the "greatest" poet of the age, Victor Hugo. González Blanco has ridiculed the excesses to which his fellow-countrymen were led by the idea of an active rivalry between the two poets. He quotes the case of Eugenio de Ochoa who related that, when in Paris, he heard Victor Hugo say that he wished to compete with the *Doloras*; the *Chansons des rues et des bois*, which appeared a year later (1865), were intended to carry out this aspiration. Evidently, Ochoa's memory or his imagination was playing tricks with him, since Hugo was absent from Paris from 1851 till 1870.[8]

Campoamor's enemies followed the opposite course of accusing him of plagiarizing Hugo. This indictment hung for years like a shadow-casting cloud over Campoamor's reputation. It burst to the accompaniment of thunder and lightning in 1876, when a series of accusing articles were published in *El Globo* over the signatures of "Vásquez" and "Nakens." Campoamor was denounced as a plagiarist, and in proof some hundred quotations from Victor Hugo were given, which the Spanish poet had copied almost literally. The admirers of Spain's most famous poet were dismayed, while his enemies rejoiced. Don Ramón felt himself lost and protested loudly that he could not even read French. The attacking forces had no difficulty in showing that this was a weak lie, and Campoamor adopted the wise course of confessing everything. As Valera says in *La originalidad y el plagio*, which he devoted to this incident:

_____

[7]*Œuvres complètes de Honoré de Balzac* (Paris: Louis Conard, 1912), VI, 223.
[8]Andrés González-Blanco, *Campoamor*, 94.

"El poeta español ha copiado al francés. El mismo ha tenido que confesarlo y lo ha confesado. Para algunos finos amantes de la literatura la reputación del Sr. Campoamor está punto menos que perdida con tal descubrimiento."[9]

The names "Vásquez" and "Nakens" were unknown, so many thought them to be pseudonyms. It was widely suggested that Valera was the real author of the articles, and some called upon Don Juan to congratulate him for having exposed an imposter. He, however, rejected the suggestion, recalling that he had written the favourable essay on Campoamor's poetry which we have already mentioned. Valera commented on the unfortunate situation which had now arisen in the following fashion:

"Las cien frases tomadas a Victor Hugo y otras ciento más que se me citen no me hacen variar de opinión, sino que sigo teniendo al Sr. Campoamor en el mismo concepto en que antes le tenía. Casi le tengo ahora en mejor concepto, porque yo no le hubiera perdonado jamás que de su propia cosecha hubiese sacado las absurdas rarezas o los pensamientos hueros é hinchados que se citan, mientras que, siendo de Víctor Hugo, ya se los perdono como una niñada disculpable" (XXIV, 72).

It is evident that Valera has his tongue in his cheek.

In the articles published in *El Globo*, Campoamor was accused likewise of plagiarizing Michelet. This indictment appeared also in the "Prefacio a manera de sinfonía" of the *Solos de Clarín*, in which the malicious Leopoldo Alas pointed out the supposed similarity between Campoamor's verses:

"como en su cuerno de marfil Rolando
gastó la fuerza hasta acabar la vida"

and the words of Michelet:

"Ce cor dans lequel il soufflait si furieusement . . . que les veines de son col en rompissent"—*Histoire de France* (Paris: Lacroix, 1879) I, 335.

One French writer whom Campoamor certainly did not imitate was Renan. The two had contradictory developments, in that the Breton was a conservative while the Asturian was a liberal, and a progressive while the Spaniard was a reactionary. After a summary trial of the ideas of Renan concerning that "absolute" which tormented so many writers of the last century, Campoamor condemns them without reprieve in *Lo absoluto* (I, 610-11).

[9] Juan Valera, *Obras completas*, XXIV, 71.

It is obvious that the Spanish writer could not study French literature so widely without being influenced in his style, which, in point of fact, shows a marked Gallic imprint. As González Blanco says:

"Campoamor fué quien despertó en nuestro país el gusto por la *boutade*, hoy tan idolatrada por ciertos jóvenes, un poco irreflexivos a veces, pero que no tienen otro defecto mayúsculo. El importó de Francia esa afición a la frase incisiva, al rasgo cortante, al chisporreteo del del ingenio."[10]

Despite an attachment of over a quarter of a century to the French language, Campoamor attempted, in his hypocritical *Discurso en la Real Academia Española*, to flatter the Francophobe reactionaries of the Academy by stupid accusations against the tongue in which he had learned to speak intellectually:

"Aparece Descartes en el siglo XVII y . . . descalvó al idioma español poniendo fin a su reinado e inauguró al mismo tiempo un destino tan glorioso como inmerecido para la lengua francesa" (I, 410).

A comparison of this *Discurso* with Rivarol's *Discours* might lead to the cynical conclusion that thought is purely relative and has little or no intrinsic value.

---

[10]*Campoamor*, 192.

CHAPTER XIII

THE WHITE RACE. CAUCASIAN BRANCH. NORTHERN GROUP.
GERMANY.

WE have now reached the summit of Campoamor's ethnological scale. The Spaniard expresses, in *El personalismo*, sincere respect for the Nordic races:

"La rama septentrional del tronco caucasiano posee un carácter tan sereno, tan firme y tan persistente que desespera con su acompasada tenacidad el destemplado ardor de sus hermanos del Mediodía. Tan característica es en éstos la agresión como en aquéllos la resistencia. Los europeos del Norte parecen los destinados por su valor, su buen sentido y su paciencia a contener en los límites de la racionalidad los disparados ímpetus de los pueblos meridionales" (I, 87-88).

It is indeed significant that a Spaniard should regard the Nordic peoples as policemen qualified to repress disorders provoked by the Mediterranean nations. Campoamor even thought that the situation would perpetually improve for the former and presumably deteriorate for the latter; the hierarchy is permanent:

"Los pueblos anglo-teutónicos, que ocupan la parte septentrional y central de Europa, seguirán ensanchando sus familias por toda la haz de la tierra, con la insistencia que les da su orgullo, con el exclusivismo que les inspira su amor proprio y con la felicidad que siempre acompaña a la inteligencia" (I, 107).

This suggestion that the Nordic peoples are outstanding for their intelligence was typical of the eighteenth and early nineteenth centuries, when England and Germany were regarded as the homes of serious thought.

Unfortunately, in Campoamor's estimation, Germany has jeopadized its position upon Olympus by its liaison with the Orient. This reproach is directed especially against Prussia. Campoamor, in his *Filosofía de las leyes*, classes the Prussian monarchy with the oriental despotisms (II, 226).

This stigma would seem more aptly applied to Russia. However, Campoamor wrote his most important works prior to the wave of Russophilia which swept away Pardo-Bazán and others, and the references to Russia in his writings are very scanty. In their "Juicio del Mundo," which is Canto XVI of *Colón* (1853), Faith, Hope, and Charity admit expectations of a world revolution beginning in Russia:

"Saludad a Moscou [sic], la ciudad santa
del cual blandón ha de incendiar un día
de los cosacos la salvaje tropa
para alumbrar la libertad de Europa" (IV, 543).

This isolated reference to Russia shows singular foresight, although it is regrettable that Faith, Hope, and Charity should be such poetasters.

French thought offered Campoamor a fundamental problem: Descartes. German history presented him with a parallel case: Luther was another of the Spaniard's obsessions. Campoamor devotes a chapter of *El personalismo* (I, 264-65) to this Anti-Christ, whom he frequently eulogizes as the liberator of the human mind. It is necessary to know Luther's reputation in Mediterranean countries to realize how striking this attitude is. Campoamor is well aware that he is playing with fire, and, in his discussions of the schismatic, he attempts to please both Greeks and Trojans:

"Desde que tengo uso de la razón estoy oyendo a los católicos decir que Lutero era un *animal* y a los libre-pensadores aseguran que era un *ángel*. ¿No podríamos partir la diferencia, colocándole en la categoría mediocre de un genio?" (I, 264).

Although Campoamor takes good care to heap reproaches on Martin Luther, they are in the main intended as a smoke-screen. The Spanish philosopher seems, fundamentally, to admire Luther for having destroyed the temporal power of the Church, yet to condemn him for having founded "*el protestantismo, ese confucismo europeo* (I, 167). This indictment of orientalizing Europe is directed by Campoamor against both Protestantism and its heir, German philosophy.

Campoamor was nourished on French though. He was by no means as amenable to German philosophy, which he considered inferior, dangerous, and arid. As he says in *El personalismo*:

"No vayan mis lectores a creer que el empirismo francés del siglo pasado se parece en nada al materialismo moderno, emanado del idealismo alemán, no: mientras que este último . . . es un materialismo radical, aspero y sin una sola fruición moral, el empirismo enciclopédico en general tiene un no sé que de vivaz, de expansivo, de espiritual, de francés" (I, 284-85).

The nebulous systems of German philosophy were an abomination to the witty and realistic Spaniard. He revealed a singular affinity with the Positivists in that he wished to make *tabula rasa* of all these exotic phantasies:

"Es menester levantar una cruzada que extermine esos espinosismos vergonzantes con que la Alemania moderna ha entontecido a medio mundo, convirtiendo a la robusta Europa en una vieja más chocha y más visionaria que la India" (I, 48).

The word *espinosismo* is significant.   Campoamor regarded Spinoza as the link between Luther and the German philosophical school.   Yet, whereas Luther had awakened the human mind, Spinoza had lulled it into a stupor:

"El pensamiento de Espinosa ha quedado en el mundo como una especie de opio atmosférico que adormece todos los entendimientos, que se ha infiltrado en todos los espacios . . . Espinosa . . . ese horno egipcio donde se han incubado todos los panteísmos que constituyen la moderna filosofía alemana" (I, 295).

It is ironical that Campoamor should accuse German philosophy of pantheism, while his Catholic enemies made exactly the same reproach against him.   It must in justice be said that the charge can with infinitely more truth be made against German philosophy than against Campoamor.   Although he regards Spinoza as a bad influence, the Spaniard places him much higher than his German successors:

"Cuando, después de haber leído a Espinosa, se quieren investigar los sucesivos sistemas filosóficos, parece que se está viendo una colección de *monos sabios* esforzándose con gesticulaciones ridículas en imitar las hercúleas acciones de un gigante" (I, 312).

German philosophy was, according to Campoamor, dragged down to its fuming inferno by Kant, the same Kant who was idolized by the Neo-Criticists and so many other philosophical groups of the nineteenth century.   Campoamor analyzes the philosophy of Kant and concludes: "No se puede emplear más talento en mayor futilidad" (I, 246).   He later discusses other aspects of Kant's philosophy and comments:

"Kant siempre me ha parecido un iluso y sus adeptos unos benditos . . . no hay crimen filosófico del cual Kant no sea autor, o, por lo menos, cómplice" (I, 303).

Campoamor disliked above all the negative, destructive, illusory character of Kant's philosophy.

We have already raised the question of the relationship between the Spaniard's *Yo* and the *Ich* of Fichte.   Campoamor was undoubtedly influenced by the German, yet he pours scorn on his egotistic system:

"El *Yo* de Fichte parece un mono ocioso y solitario haciendo muecas enfrente de un espejo, y, después de estudiado el conjunto de todos sus gestos y todas sus actitudes, sólo se saca por consecuencia que el *Yo* de Fichte, que el sistema del *idealismo transcendental* es el gran caricato de la farsa de este mundo" (I, 307).

Fichte seemed to Campoamor to be personally ridiculous. He says that, if he had attended the famous lecture which Fichte ended with the words "In the next lesson we will create God," he would have done from laughter what Saint Ehpraim did from fear whenever he thought of the Last Judgment: namely, fainted outright (I, 305-6).

Schelling is treated with scarcely more generosity. When he wrote *El personalismo*, Campoamor, who was later to devote a book to the absolute, rejected as meaningless that absolute in which Schelling united the ego and the non-ego, and which lay in the Divinity:

"¿Y qué es lo *absoluto?* Son muy varias las formas dadas por Schelling para hacerlo comprender, unas veces poéticas, otras contradictorias y todas ininteligibles" (I, 308).

Seldom in discussing German philosophy does Campoamor moderate his language, but toward none of its exponents is he as brutal as toward Hegel, at least in *El personalismo*:

"Me es el autor más antipático de todos los filósofos del mundo. Siempre me ha parecido risible ver a sus innumerables adeptos ocuparse del sistema de Hegel con toda formalidad. . . . Hegel es el gran mistificador del género humano. La mayor parte de las veces no sólo no sabe lo que dice, sino que sabe que no lo sabe" (I, 313).

Campoamor proceeds to analyze at length the philosophy of Hegel and to suggest, in all seriousness, that Hegel was wittingly hoodwinking his followers. Some of this animus is to be explained by the vogue which Hegel was enjoying in Campoamor's time. To this favour, above all, the Spaniard attributes, as we shall see, the impending degeneration of German thought and civilization.

Francophile and anti-theological Goethe stood a better chance of pleasing Campoamor, but the Spaniard tars him with the same brush, reproaching him for his pagan sensuality and his neo-classicism. To Goethe's boutade that four things were intolerable to him, namely tobacco, church-bells, bugs and Christianity, Campoamor retorts:

"Esta fanfarronada de Goethe, de este Juliano de las letras y las artes, de este matón de la literatura, de este guapo de la filosofía, me es a mi también más insoportable que el humo del tabaco" (I, 265-66).[1]

Apparently Campoamor was un-Spanish enough to dislike tobacco. He proceeds to arraign Jupiter, Apollo, Diana, and Venus, whom he depicts as monsters of iniquity.

Resuming all his detailed criticisms of German idealism, Campoamor condemns it as oriental, naïve, and fantastic:

"Esta existencia abstracta, anterior a todo sujeto, ya se llama *substancia* como en Espinosa, *yo* como en Fichte, absoluto como en Schelling o *idea* en Hegel, siempre es el panteísmo indiano mezclado con las más groseras creencias de la escuela jónica. Estas quimeras intelectuales no son más que representaciones místicas de la *materia eterna e increada* de Thales y Anaxágoras" (I, 322).

This remark would do credit to a militant positivist. We have already explained Campoamor's equivocal position in this matter.

The Spaniard crowns his condemnation of German philosophy with a prophecy of the end of the intellectual predominance of Germany:

"No es difícil prever la caída del imperio filosófico de la Alemania moderna. . . . Después de tan alta degradación de la ciencia filosófica, sólo falta en emperador Justiniano que mande cerrar las aulas, como si fuesen boticas donde se confeccionan potingues para envenenar el sentido común" (I, 326).

Campoamor did not realize how unhappily prophetic his words would be, how, eighty years after he wrote these lines, Germany would turn her back on her philosophical past, condemn academic activities as byzantine, and reduce universities to the rôle of technical schools.

Likewise, with amazing foresight, Campoamor predicted the trend which German politics would take as the result of the contagious Hegelian philosophy:

"Para Hegel no hay más individuo que el *hombre colectivo*. . . . De esta *antropolotría*, o sea el culto del hombre colectivo, se deduce el autocratismo más ciego, más irracional y más desenfrenado que puede degradar a la especie humana. Así el hegeliano señor Eichborn [sic][2], ministro del rey de Prusia, declaraba terminantemente, en nombre de su maestro, que 'solo al Rey pertenecía el derecho y el poder de regular la conciencia de sus vasallos.' De este modo, ese sér abstracto que

---

[1] Campoamor is unjust. *Vide* G. Keuchel, *Goethe's Religion* (Riga: Jonck, 1899).

[2] Presumably Campoamor is referring to Johann A. F. Eichhorn (1779-1856), who n 1840 became Prussian *Kultusminister*.

se llamo Estado es un gran cementerio, en el cual los cadáveres mudan de fosa según la voluntad de su representante el guardián enterrador" (I, 326-27).

It is a great tribute to the perspicacity of Campoamor that he should have perceived so clearly the latent virus of totalitarianism in Germany.

Not even the religious implications of Neo-Hegelianism escaped the Spanish Cassandra whose unheeded prophecies are, after a long lapse of time, receiving ample substantiation: he enumerates, in *El personalismo* (I, 328-29), a number of isolated phenomena which indicated that Germany was destined to become a pagan, anti-Christian country. Campoamor's black-list is headed by the *"Anales Germánicos,"*[3] *"eco de esta tropa de verdugos de todas las esperanzas humanas."* Its editors proposed as their main object, so Campoamor tells us, the extirpation and dissolution of the Christian principle, and, above all, of its three fundamental ideas, namely:

1. The idea of a conscious God distinct from the universe.
2. The idea of a historical Christ.
3. The idea of a continuation of personal existence after death.

"Estos Erostratos desboacdos," cries Campoamor, *"sin ansia de immortalidad, no sólo pegan fuego al templo del cristianismo, sino al deísmo, a la moralidad, al sentimentalismo."* Strauss denied the historicity of Christ, Bauer sought to destroy the historical authority of the Gospels,[4] Feuerbach proclaimed his unbridled hatred against the very idea of God.[5] The poetaster Herweg developed the principles of liberty and equality, and concluded by advocating licentiousness and social levelling[6] (which obviously could not appeal to Campoamor, the apostle of a social hierarchy). Professor Wilhelm Marr taught in his lectures that the dogmas

---

[3]Presumably, Campoamor is referring to the *Deutsche Annalen zur Kentniss der Gegenwart*. It began appearing in 1853 as a continuation of *Germania*, which had been published since 1836. The recent change in name explains Campoamor's use of the word *"germánicos."*

[4]Bruno Bauer (1809-1882) published in 1840 his *Kritik der Evang. Geschichte des Johannes* and his *Kritik der Evang. Synoptiker*, and in 1850 his *Kritik der Evangelien*.

[5]Ludwig Feuerbach (1804-1872) was a representative of *"Junghegelianismus,"* that is to say of the radical disciples of Hegel who fought the conservative and Christian interpretation of Hegel's philosophy. His most important work, to which Campoamor is no doubt referring, is *Das Wesen des Christentums* (1840). However, Campoamor somewhat misrepresents his attitude.

[6]Georg Herwegh (1817-1875) was a revolutionary and a socialist, but he did not deserve to be so brutally condemned.

of the existence of God and of the immortality of soul were nothing but fairy tales, and asked when the day would come that we should be free from this petty morality and from this annoying virtue. Campoamor comments with a typical witticism:

"Aunque no creo, como el profesor Marr, que 'la venganza es un acto de justicia natural,' creo que, si él leyera en mi presencia semejantes baladronadas, no podría dejar de tirarle el libro a la cabeza" (I, 328-29).

The humour may be ineffective, but that does not impair Campoamor's historical and social perspicacity.

Another proof of this clearsightedness is to be found in the prophecies which, likewise in *El personalismo*, Campoamor makes regarding the future of Austro-Hungary:

"Cada raza del imperio austríaco concluirá por constituirse en una nacionalidad independiente, estableciendo un gobierno en completa armonía con sus inclinaciones y sus necesidades" (I, 143).

Admittedly, the Great War and President Wilson were needed as a catalytic for this development, which Mazzini, before Campoamor, had predicted, but the fact remains that the prophecy has come true.

After the overwhelming attack on Germany in *El personalismo*, even an impartial spectator is disgusted with the eulogies of Germany, which Campoamor included in his *Discurso* in order to please the Germanophile reactionaries of the Academy:

"En Alemania . . . viene Kant, tan grande como Aristóteles, y acabando de desentecar el alemán, llegan a hacerle casi rival del griego, en literatura, sus adeptos Schiller y Goethe, y en filosofía un sinnúmero de discípulos" (I, 411).

In *Lo absoluto*, where he has frequent occasion to discuss German philosophy, Campoamor follows a middle path. He displays no hostiliity toward Germany, but criticizes German philosophy which, on account of its non-Catholic character, even Germanophile Spaniards regard with suspicion.

The holocaust of 1870 nauseated Campoamor and produced in him a revulsion against the militarization of Germany. The liberal awoke and expressed his indignation, admittedly in wretched doggerel, through the mouth of Victor, one of the protagonists of the poem "Guerra a la guerra":

"¿Quién podía calcular
que había de hacer Bismarck
de la Alemania un cuartel?
¿Como ha podido sacar
de entre sabios alemanes
todo un millón de jayanes
el gran canciller Bismarck?
Todo con gente lo allana;
y Molkte usa en su ambición
la táctica del cañón,
fuego contra carne humana.
Ya no hay ciencia militar:
quien consigue la victoria
no es el genio de la gloria,
es la *industria de matar*" (VI, 29).

It is fitting that Campoamor's attitude toward Germany should be discussed in chapter xiii.

CHAPTER XIV

THE blond Anglo-Saxons form the nitid apex of Campoamor's racial scale, the other end of which is occupied by the lowest type of negro. The hierarchy descends, says Campoamor in *El personalismo, "desde los anglo-sajones, semidioses del género humano, hasta las casi-cosas de los bozales de Angola"* (I, 69). By the Anglo-Saxons, Campoamor means the English, and above all those of Norman extraction. There are slight but admiring references to the Scandinavians, who, according to Campoamor's chromatic scale, should be racial models. Whereas today there is a cult of Sweden, around the middle of the last century Scandinavia was relatively unknown. For the United States, Campoamor has scarcely a favourable comment, although he was writing long before the wave of Yankeephobia which swept Spain as a result of the War of 1898. This would seem to be illogical from the standpoint of Campoamor's race theory, but he would doubtless argue that, just as Germany has degenerated through orientalization, so the United States has been contaminated by the idea of Liberty, Fraternity, and Equality. As we shall see, the liberal Campoamor of *El personalismo* did not consider even England free from that taint. Indeed, as he became old and reactionary, his admiration for England turned into hatred.

Although the Campoamor of *El personalismo* hated Equality, he was a fervent devotee of Liberty. The historic importance of England, according to the Spaniard, is that it has safeguarded the ideal of freedom for the peoples of the world: He does not hesitate to affirm that even Spain is indebted to Albion in this respect:

> "Las libertades civiles, que los españoles con tanto entusiasmo defendieron en el siglo xvi, cayeron en desuso por una reacción atónica de su ardor meridional; mientras que los ingleses, después de la carta hecha firmar a Juan Sin-Tierra, contuvieron con una patriótica pertinacia las caprichosas voluntariedades de las testas coronadas, y con su ejemplo emanciparon a las sociedades de las egoístas exigencias del derecho divino de los reyes" (I, 88).

The twin sister of English liberty is English democracy, which antidemocratic Campoamor should have despised, but which he nevertheless admitted and admired, because it was a disguised form of aristocracy, with a social hierarchy:

> "Admiro las antiguas democracias a la *espartana*, a la *romana*, a la

inglesa, con sus clases privilegiadas, sus siérvos, sus esclavos y sus proletarios" (I, 152).

It must be remembered that England had still not adopted universal suffrage.

It would be logical, therefore, to expect Campoamor to admire the British aristocracy. However, the devotee of intelligence wanted a hierarchy based solely on merit. The traditional nobility of Europe irked him—this very irritation explains why later Campoamor tried to solve the difficulty by associating himself with nobility—and the English peerage represented the most outstanding example of the system. In *El personalismo*, the advocate of a merit-system tells us:

"La vanidad de las noblezas modernas de casi todas las naciones de Europa es ridícula, porque sus nobles son grandes por convención. Los gobiernos aristocráticos de Roma y de la Gran Bretaña han hecho y hacen sentir al mundo los efectos de un intolerable orgullo; el de Roma con los privilegios y tradiciones senatoriales de sus patricios, y el de Inglaterra con las linajadas preocupaciones y bruscos arranques de sus barones y sus lores" (I, 204-5).

This system seemed nonetheless to Campoamor infinitely preferable to absolute social equality, and when Castelar boasted with the satisfaction of a democrat:

"Inglaterra ve desplomarse poco a poco su antigua aristocracia,"

Campoamor retorted, in his *Polémicas con la democracia*:

"Cierto. Por eso se va desplomando poco a poco su antiguo poder" (I, 537).

It is scarcely possible to find a year from 1763 to the present day when some grave prophet has not pronounced England to be irrevocably decadent.

Although an imitator—some would say a plagiarist—of Victor Hugo, Campoamor devotes little time or space to the theme of humanitarianism. Yet, in Hugoesque phrases, he eulogizes English public welfare as a proof of the progress that humanity has made since ancient times:

"En los tiempos heroicos de Lacedemonia, los jóvenes de Esparta Esparta salían a los campos a degollar a los inermes islotas, con el objeto de ensayarse para las guerras; mientras que hoy el gobierno inglés extiende su ternura a diez mil desamparados, que diariamente se acogen a su caridad en las largas y encrudecidas noches del invierno en los lugares de asilo, en cuyas puertas se hallan escritas estas consoladoras palabras del Evangelio: Llamad y se os abrirá" (I, 95).

This passage from *El personalismo* smacks of Christian Socialism. It is needless to say that, in his reactionary period, Campoamor avoided any such generous remarks.

The Spaniard who, in principle, despised the black race and thought slavery a quite defensible institution, forgot himself in his eulogies of English humanitarianism and praised the British government for its abolitionist efforts:

"Haciendo entender la ley de Cristo en su expresión más lata y más genuina, emplea su colosal poder en abolir la esclavitud, llevando la libertad y la igualdad posibles hasta a los seres más abyectos de la península africana" (I, 95).

Campoamor seems to have had little more than a nodding acquaintance with English literature. He expresses with a happy metaphor, in *El personalismo*, his nebulous admiration for Shakespeare:

"El audaz Shakespeare, para quien el corazón humano era un océano inmenso donde siempre encontraba islas desconocidas de los demás hombres" (I, 188).

Later, in his *Poética* (1883), Campoamor made a comparison between English and Spanish humour. This comparison, which has become a commonplace of subsequent critics, would seem to owe its origin to Campoamor:

"La frase *buen humor*, genuínamente española, ha creado un género literario, que es sólo peculiar de los ingleses y de los españoles, y en el que, mezclando lo alegre con lo trágico, se forma un tejido de luz y sombra, al través del cual se ve en perspectiva flageladas las grandezas y sanctificadas las miserias, produciendo esta mezcla del llanto y de la risa una sobreexcitación de un encanto indefinible. El humorismo francés es satírico, el italiano burlesco y el alemán elegíaco. Sólo Cervantes y Shakespeare son los dos tipos del verdadero humorismo, serio, ingenuo y candoroso" (III, 240).

The rôle of English philosophy in the intellectual development of Campoamor exactly parallels that of French thought, both being antithetical to German metaphysics. In *El personalismo* (I, 354), Campoamor includes England among the "intelligent, energetic, personal, and superior peoples" who have shown a healthy skepticism toward speculative philosophy of the German type. This is clearly a reference to the tradition of Locke, Hume, and Spencer.

English science is the brilliant justification of philosophical skepticism. One of the idols of liberal Campoamor was Newton. Addressing speculative philosophers, he says:

"La manzana de Newton ha hecho a Dios más grande que todos vuestros cuentos de hada" (I, 27).

He quotes with reverence the dying remarks of Newton (I, 94).

Campoamor's change from a progressive to a conservative viewpoint is evident in his essay *Bacon* (1857). True to his liberalism, he begins by defending Bacon against De Maistre:

"¿Qué razón pudo tener M. Maistre, ese inquisidor literario, para calificar de ateao, inmoral, impío y padre de todos los errores a un hombre tan circunspecto en política y tan cuerdo en la moral[1] y al cual somos deudores de máximas como la presente: 'Un poco de filosofía natural hace inclinar los hombres hacia el ateísmo; un conocimiento más profundo de esta ciencia los vuelve la religión'....[2] empezó Bacon a escribir contra Aristóteles, teniéndole, con justa razón, por el padre de la filosofía escolástica, de ese inmenso pecado de la ociosidad" (I, 694-95).

The essay slowly develops into an attack on the Bacon idolized by Voltaire and the Encyclopedists.[3] Campoamor concludes by condemning the inductive method as incapable of reaching God, and placing it on a distinctly inferior plane to "*el alma, el Yo, la personalidad, en fin, que por un método completamente antibaconiano ha sido creada por gracia de Dios y para gloria de los hombres* (I, 702). The attack on Macaulay in *La metafísica y la poesía* (1891) is indirectly a condemnation of Bacon.

Campoamor's reaction against English positivistic thought is illustrated in the tirade which he hurls at Spencer in *El ideísmo*:

"Dos volúmenes de psicología,[4] que en el fondo son una mala fisiología, emplea Spencer en hacer preludios tocando los nervios de personas y de cosas material y fisiológicamente, para hacer creer que está ejecutando arpegios anímicos, cuando aquel toqueteo mecánico sólo produce una música sin melodía y sin alma" (III, 417).

This metaphor was possibly inspired by the Leopoldo Alas of *Solos de Clarín*. Be that as it may, the modernistic melodies of Spencer constantly grated on Campoamor's ears during his reactionary period.

---

[1] Joseph de Maistre condemns Bacon in the "Cinquième entretien" of his *Soirées de Saint-Pétersbourg*; he treats Locke even more harshly in the following *Entretien*.

[2] Campoamor is translating a dictum which occurs in Bacon's essay "Of Atheism": "A little philosophy inclineth man's mind to atheism, but depth in philosophy bringeth men's minds about to religion."

[3] *E.g.* Voltaire, *Dictionnaire philosophique*, art. "Bacon (François)."

[4] Herbert Spencer, *Principles of Psychology*. The first edition (1855) had one volume, the second (1872), two.

In brief, then, Campoamor was extremely favorable toward England until he became a die-hard defender of Hispanity, when he remembered that Albion was the land of Drake and of his heretical seed.

Toward the young and immature United States, Campoamor was indifferent during his liberal period. He was, however, not actively hostile, and he made, for example, a flattering reference to Franklin (I, 27).

During his reactionary period, he came to despise America as the land of the Almighty Dollar, where the only values are economic. He asks in *Polémicas con la democracia*:

> "¿Como quiere el señor Rodríguez[5] que no pueda mirar sin *desprecio* una doctrina social cuyo catecismo económico, redactado por un norteamericano, se puede reducir a estas cinco preguntas y respuestas?
> ¿Qué es la vida?
> Un tiempo fijado para ganar dinero.
> ¿Qué es dinero?
> El objeta de la vida.
> ¿Y el hombre?
> Una máquina de ganar dinero.
> ¿Y la mujer?
> Una máquina de gastar dinero.
> ¿Y los hijos?
> Una semilla que produce máquinas para ganar o gastar dinero."
> (II, 430-31).

Campoamor heard of Mormonism but failed completely to understand or do justice to the spirit of the movement. Like many Catholics, as, for example, Pierre Benoît in his novel *Le Lac Salé* (1921), he regarded it as a typically American combination of money-seeking and pleasure lust. In *Polémicas con la democracia*, he formulates thus the dogma of Mormonism:

> "Trabajad y gozad; sed ricos y no penséis más que en satisfacer vuestras pasiones" (II, 637-38).

For reactionary Campoamor, the worst form of that repugnant thing, democracy, was the American variety, since social hierarchy had disappeared from the equalitarian United States. Despairing at the triumph of Napoleon III in France, Castelar exclaimed:

---

[5]Gabriel Rodríguez (1827-1901); a noted economist, for long years represented Puerto Rico in the Spanish congress, and was sympathetic toward the democracy of the United States.

"Allá en el Atlántico se levanta un mundo en el cual sólo es posible la libertad, mundo más hermoso que la antigua Europa, preparado por Dios para una nueva idea, para la idea democrática."

Campoamor retorted, in his *Polémicas con la democracia* (II, 536), with a number of disparaging references to the United States, *"esa nación sin rey ni Roque."* This argument was vented just before the American Civil War, so that Campoamor was able to comment:

"En esta nación de nacioncillas [unpleasantly similar to the federal system advocated for Spain by the school of Pi y Margall], es donde dice al señor Castelar que sólo es posible la *libertad*, cuando actualmente es el único país del mundo donde sólo es posible la esclavitud" (II, 536-67).

The only civilized country, Campoamor should have said, for slavery had certainly not been eradicated from the whole world. Moreover, Campoamor's use of the word *actualmente* is historically ironical; he failed to foresee the outbreak of the Civil War a few years later, and the consequent abolition of slavery in the United States. Castelar, in any case, was clearly thinking of the Northern States.

In contrast with his remarkably clear-sighted vision of the latent development of Germany, Campoamor shows a lamentable obtuseness regarding the future of the United States.

CHAPTER XV

SPAIN

IN analyzing Campoamor's ethnographical hierarchy from the bottom to the top, we pointed out Spain's place among the Mediterranean nations but decided to wait until the whole of the outside world had been described before discussing the Peninsula.

Like most of the writers who have devoted their attention to the problem of Spain and the world, Campoamor is impressed and depressed by the aura of tragedy which surrounds the whole matter. Following his tendency to stress the importance of race, Campoamor attributes the unhappy fate of his country to the heterogeneous elements which compose its population. This would seem to be in addition to the fact that the Spanish people, belonging to the mercurial Mediterranean race, are naturally unstable. The following lines from *El personalismo* have a tragic sincerity:

"Si una nación como la española se compone de castas antitéticas por su organización, entonces su historia es una representación teatral llena de peripecias. La energía y la debilidad, la dignidad y la anarquía, la inteligencia y la ignorancia son personajes que siempre salen al escenario, aunque salen cuando menos se les espera. La historia de España es una comedia de capa y espada, donde las bufonadas del sainete se hallan mezcladas con los terrores de la tragedia, y en la cual siempre son complicados los enredos y siempre los desenlaces son inesperados" (I, 142).

What of the Golden Age? Tinsel and blood-stained steel, replies Campoamor. In the best tradition of the *leyenda negra*, he affirms in *El personalismo*:

"Cuando los españoles espaciaron su energía física y moral por una gran parte del mundo antiguo y por todo el hemisferio occidental del globo, extremaron su crueldad y su soberbia hasta un punto que hará extremecer de horror a cuantas generaciones llegue la historia fiel de sus novelescas hazañas" (I, 87).

Contrast this with Pardo-Bazán's cult of Hernán Cortés and her complete lack of shame for his "crimes."

It is easy to see what elements of the civilization of the Golden Age were distasteful to Campoamor. He hated above all its theology and its mysticism. Yet, whatever his theoretical attitude toward asceticism, he never freed himself completely from the ascetic tradition. *El per-*

sonalismo, in general a decidedly anti-traditionalist book, ends with a eulogy of those who have resisted pleasure and remained innocent. It makes quaint reading:

> "¡ . . . Madres que concebisteis sin más voluptuosidad que la del cumplimiento de un deber!" . . . (I, 253).

Campoamor expounded an idea which, in more recent times, has been much favoured by Spanish radical writers: namely, that the arch-Catholic Spain of the Golden Age was, below the surface, riddled with protestantism. This is exemplified in Juan García, the canon and doctor of Barcelona prominent in the poem *El Licenciado Torralba*:

> "García, aunque católico romano,
> ya prefiere, un poquito luterano,
> al criterio de Roma, la Escritura,
> y formando una ley de su conciencia,
> se confiesa con Dios, que es buen cura
> que oye, calla y no impone penitencia" (VII, 625).

El Licenciado Torralba himself, who is in some measure a personification of Campoamor, is condemned, at the end of the poem, as a protestant and, worse still, a deist:

> "*Constando* que, causando su entusiasmo
> Martín Lutero y Desiderio Erasmo,
> sólo ama la materia, y de este modo
> su ciencia es tan profana
> que, odiando el alma humana,
> admira el alma cósmica del todo;
> *Constando* que este monstruo de impostura
> para un cercano porvenir augura
> la religión del Padre
> sin Hijo, sin Espíritu y sin Madre;
> *Constando* que, según su testimonio,
> el Dios-Hijo fué un hombre extraordinario;
> y que a veces también, el temerario,
> dudó de la existencia del demonio;
> por el cielo inspirado
> el Tribunal acuerda
> que a Eugenio de Torralba, al Licenciado
> se le aplique el tormento de la cuerda" (VII, 643).

For Campoamor, the rôle of the Holy Office was no mere historical or academic question. Recalling his own experiences, he denounces in *El personalismo* the ever-living spirit of the Inquisition:

"No sólo en mi primera edad, sino que también en mi edad adulta los efectos inquisitoriales de un catolicismo mal entendido han venido a exacerbarme hasta en lo que hay de más íntimo en la vida" (I, 259).

Campoamor's cry recalls, in a minor, anguished key, Goethe's death-bed appeal for more light:

"Desde que he nacido me tienen aprisionado. ¡Aire, que me ahogo!" (I, 283).

The aforegoing considerations would imply that Campoamor had no sympathy, at least in his liberal period, for the powers that were, in the Spain of the so-called Golden Age. He condemns Jiménez de Cisneros as a fanatic for having burned in Granada five thousand volumes containing the unsurpassed progress made by the Arabs in agriculture and medicine (I, 225).[1]

Had Campoamor been consistent, he would have excoriated with equal vigour the cardinal's sponsor, Isabel the Catholic. Yet, although a skeptic and an iconoclast, he has penned, a few pages later, a eulogy of the Catholic Queen which would do justice to the most naïve traditionalist. It begins hyperbolically:

"Esta señora es el carácter más bello y más grande que honra la historia del linaje humano" (I, 241).

Campoamor seems to lose temporarily his sense of humour, as when he praises the lady's modesty:

"Símbolo del pudor, encargó con mucha eficacia que no la descubriesen los pies para ponerle la Extremaunción en aquel terrible y augusto momento en que parece que el alma se recoge en el seno de la eternidad, abandonando toda idea de la tierra" (I, 242).

Campoamor gives Isabel particular praise for sponsoring the project of Columbus.

He does not extend his monarchist's reverence to Charles V. This is but natural, since Spaniards have always regarded the emperor as at least half a foreigner, whereas Isabel the Catholic and Philip II are deemed untainted in their Hispanity. Campoamor always injects a dose of irony into his references to Carlos Quinto. The emperor is the

---

[1]Cisneros did save two or three hundred medical works, which he caused to be transferred to his new university at Alcalá. *Vide* Reginald Merton, *Cardinal Ximenes and the Making of Spain* (London: Kegan Paul, 1934), 77.

subject of two satirical *doloras*, "Los grandes hombres" (V, 210-12), which relates the emperor's mock funeral at Yuste,[2] and "Los relojes del Rey Carlos" (V, 213-15), which ridicules his mania for collecting clocks.[3] In the *dolora*, "El candil de Carlos V," Campoamor expresses his amusement at the great monarch who would delight in a duel with Francis I, but who was afraid of the draughts at Yuste (V, 354). The mock epic, "La gloria de las Austrias" (in *Los pequeños poemas*) is another satirical picture of the life of Charles V at Yuste. A line in the last strophe, "*Y, siendo algo español el gran Tudesco*" (VIII, 438) is significant and contains the explanation of the indifference of Campoamor and his fellow-countrymen toward the emperor.

The propagators of "*la leyenda negra*" had succeeded in persuading the world that Philip II was a monster of iniquity. The Neo-Catholics undertook to rehabilitate him, proclaiming that "*el demonio del Mediodía*" was indeed a saint. In *El personalismo* (I, 229), Campoamor expresses indifference regarding this controversy and suggests that archæological interest in the Escorial was largely responsible for the growing sympathy toward Philip. In a subsequent chapter, he illustrates his analysis of the human passions with a reference to "*un hombre tan vehemente y tan fanático como Felipe II*" (I, 240).

Later, in his reactionary period, Campoamor came to idealize Felipe II as a great king defeated in a struggle with overwhelming circumstances:

> "Es común entre los historiadores empíricos echar la culpa a este rey excepcional de que el fué el primer causante de la ruína del inmenso imperio español. ¡Bah! Es cierto que aquel gran político no podía tener herederos que continuasen su obra sin que la naturaleza se hubiese excedido a sí misma, pero el imperio español no podía menos de derrumbarse desde que se establecieron los ejércitos permanentes y desde que no pudimos batirnos tantos a tantos, sino que las demás naciones se hicieron superiores a nosotros por el mayor número de soldados. En cuestiones de fuerza bruta, la fuerza bruta es lo primero" (III, 515).

This passage from *El ideísmo* is really a vindication not only of Philip II, but also his successors, the third and fourth of the same name. Campoamor suggests, then, that there never was any decadence of Spain, nor

---

[2]Historians consider this to be a legend. *Vide* Christopher Hare, *A Great Emperor: Charles V* (New York: Scribner's, 1917) pp. 313-14.

[3]Charles was not such a maniac as Campoamor suggests. *Vide* M. Mignet, *Charles-Quint. Son abdication, son séjour et sa mort au Monastère de Yuste* (Paris: Paulin Lheureux, 1854), 216.

any defeat by intellectual or moral forces, but mere oppression by sheer weight of numbers. This argument puts Spain in the heroic position of a martyr, but it is redolent with wishful thinking.

In the same work, *El ideísmo*, there is a fulsome panegyric of Spain's great trinity of monarchs: Isabel the Catholic—there is no mention of her Aragonese husband, whom good Castilian conservatives do not like —Charles V—who is included no doubt for the sake of symmetry— and Philip II:

"No hay ejemplo en la historia de una trinidad más gloriosa de reyes que aquélla de Isabel la Católica, que se despojó de sus alhajas para que Colón pudiese descubrir nuevos mundos que hiciesen más numerosa la comunión de las fieles, del inmortal Carlos V, que, luchando con pueblos y con príncipes, se expuso a divorciarse de la buena fortuna, según él decía, *como mujer poco amiga de los viejos*, por defender la fe heredada de su ilustre abuela, y de Felipe II, que, teniendo un entendimiento más vasto que su reino universal [!], a pesar de sus lógicas inconsecuencias, fué más ideal y sufrió más por la señora de sus pensamientos que el más perfecto de los caballeros legendarios, batiéndose por ella por mar y por tierra, en España, en Italia, en Francia, en Inglaterra, en Africa, en América, y en la Oceanía" (III, 514).

This is the usual conservative interpretation of Spanish history as one unending, heroic, and disinterested crusade on behalf of the Catholic faith.

There have, in recent years, been several attempts to vindicate the memory of Philip IV. Apart from this, he has always been regarded as a black sheep, even by staunch monarchists, and Campoamor never dared, in his most fervent traditionalist moods, to include him declaredly in the glorious line of Spanish kings. In the monster-poem *El drama universal* (1869), reminiscent of the *Divine Comedy*, Philip IV and his suite are grouped among those damned for "El pecado de la pereza," which is the title of the *escena* in which their plight is described (xxvii):

"Tan bravos infanzones, convirtiendo
a la pereza en su deidad querida,
haciendo sólo tiempo, van haciendo
un eterno bostezo de la vida.

Allí al ciego querer de la fortuna
Felipe IV, el español, se entrega,
y jamás llega a tiempo a parte alguna
esperando una cosa que no llega.

Vasallos dignos de él le van siguiendo,
que holgando hacen al rey digno agasajo,
y más que en trabajar, sufren huyendo
del que llaman demonio del trabajo" (VII, 283).

So much for the *Zeitgeist* and the politics of the Golden Age. What of its culture? Even in his iconoclastic youth, Campoamor never descended to the indignity of suggesting that the *Quijote* was not, in every respect, a superhuman work. He has the good manners to class Cervantes, in *El personalismo*, with Homer and Plato:

"En el orden intelectual, Homero fija el tipo de la perfecta idealidad; Platón inficiona la humanidad de un *iluminismo*, cuyo último rayo se extinguirá el último día del mundo; Cervantes, en su *Quijote*, hizo el epitafio más impío de la edad caballeresca y la introducción más sublime de la civilización moderna" (I, 139).

Thus Campoamor, in his youth, appreciated the *Quijote* as an iconoclastic work. In his reactionary period, he no doubt admired it for its untainted Hispanity. Spanish critics find it possible to admire the *Quijote* from every conceivable angle.

Campoamor shows more discernment in his criticism of the poetry of the Golden Age. Replying to Lista, who maintained that the language of poetry must be different from that of prose, and that Fernando de Herrera had set a standard for Spain in this respect,[4] our hater of conventional poetry declares, in his *Poética*, that he much prefers the unaffected language of Jorge Manrique and of his followers, Garcilaso, Fray Luis de León, and Lope de Vega.

During his anti-traditionalist years, Campoamor had no interest in the theological literature of the Golden Age. He makes, in *El personalismo*, a disparaging reference to:

"Santa Teresa de Jesús, redactando sus cartas apasionadas y empleando los efusivos arranques de su espíritu en mistificar visiones halagüeñas" (I, 241).

In his subsequent conservative period, Campoamor changed completely in this respect. Defending himself against the charge of plagiarism, in *La originalidad y el plagio*, which was originally a letter dated December, 1875, and addressed to Fernández Bremón,[5] he speaks with reverence of Calderón de la Barca, affirming that *La vida es sueño*,

---

[4] *Vide* Alberto Lista, "Del lenguage poético," *Artículos críticos y literarios* (Palma: Estevan Trias, 1840), I, 78 ff.

[5] José Fernández Bremón (1839-1910), journalist and author.

despite all it owes to previous works, is *"la obra más grande de que hacen mención los anales del espíritu humano"* (III, 201). It would not be unjust to describe this praise as hyperbolic.

The liberal Campoamor of *El personalismo* should have realized that he was following directly the tradition of Aranda, Quintana, Larra, and the other representatives of the Spanish *Aufklärung*. However, he makes practically no reference to them. Admittedly, he drew his inspiration, not through them, but directly from French sources.

Later, in his Prologue to the *Dudas y tristezas* (1875) of Manuel de la Revilla, he makes a merciless attack on Quintana:

"La mayor parte de sus asuntos, como la *propagación de la vacuna*, por ejemplo, son más propios de una Revista hebdomadaria que para ser cantados por la lira de un poeta. Los planes de sus composiciones nunca son dramáticos; están lo que se llama mal compuestos; excepto en dos o tres composiciones, jamás saca actores a la escena para que el lector vea clara y pictóricamente lo que se propone decir o representar. Su arranque patriótico, violentado para hacerlo aplicable a nuestras luchas políticas contemporáneas, más que patriotismo es un verdadero patrioterismo, y aunque a un poeta se le puede perdonar hasta que falsifique la historia, como en 'El Panteón del Escorial' y diga cosas tan injustas como sus diatribas contra el Papado, lo que no es disculpable es que, después de presentarse al público con dos docenas de composiciones escogidas, como si él fuese un ingenio de naturalera [sic] olímpica que no ha tenido jamás debilidades poéticas como los demás mortales, no tenga entre todas ellas dos docenas de imágenes nuevas, sencillas, y pintorescas" (III, 24-25).

A special study would be necessary to describe in any detail Campoamor's attitude toward the personalities and problems of his age. Only a brief summary is possible here. The most constant theme of this subject is Campoamor's faithfulness to the liberal monarchy, in particular to María Cristina. He was certainly no time-server, for he was most loud in his praise of the queen when she was in general disfavor. When María Cristina was exiled in 1840, he composed a bilious ode entitled "A la Reina Cristina restauradora de las libertades patrias al partir para su destierro." The young poet wags a reproachful finger at Spain:

"En buen hora con saña
solemnices en órgia placentera
tu criminal hazaña:
¡gloria al león de España
que el pecho hirió de una infeliz cordera!

Engríe tus pendones
agobiados de bélicas coronas
quien venció Napoleones
añada a sus blasones
la baja prez de proscribir matronas" (IV, 249).

On María Cristina's return, he greeted her with a similar ode, "Al regreso de S.M. la Reina Doña María Cristina" (IV, 250-51). Just over a decade later, in 1854, María Cristina was once more exiled, this time irrevocably. In *El personalismo*, which appeared a year later (1855), Campoamor, now more mature, expressed his feelings in more measured and less fiery terms. Recalling the aforementioned ode which he dedicated to María Cristina on the occasion of her exile, he comments:

"No haría mención de este hecho, si no fuera porque hoy, que se halla desterrada como entonces, es impopular el exaltecer sus merecimientos. . . . En esta patria de las grandes reinas, la reina Cristina será en la historia una de las más grandes" (I, 336).[6]

Likewise, but without displaying the same enthusiasm, Campoamor was a faithful subject of Isabel II. He addressed to her the poetry-less poem "Quien perdona, a Dios merece," which begins:

"No habrá español que hoy día
la sien ceñida de gloriosa palma
no os cante, Reina mía
con los sones más íntimos del alma "(IV, 306).

Looking back on the reign of Isabel II, Campoamor, writing in 1873, did not hesitate to describe it, in the "Advertencia" which he added to the second edition of *Polémicas con la democracia*, as *"uno de los más gloriosos de que hará mención la historia del género humano"* (II, 662). This simple phrase reveals that blind megalomania of Spanish traditionalists which led them to undertake with naïve optimism a war against the United States.

For the last quarter of a century of his life, Campoamor was a staunch supporter of the restored monarch, Alfonso XII. He had already dedicated to him, in 1860, while he was Prince of Asturias, the *dolora* "Los dos cetros," in which he counselled the future king to imitate his mother:

"Noble, cual vuestra nación
a vuestra madre imitad

---

[6] *Vide* Edmund B. d'Auvergne, *A Queen at Bay* (London: Hutchinson, 1910), chaps. xii and xvi.

> en cuyo Real corazón
> se aman justicia y perdón
> se abrazan dicha y verdad" (V, 248).

When Alfonso XII ascended his uneasy throne, he could wish for no more loyal subject than Campoamor. It is significant that it was our poet who made a speech in the Cortes on January 10, 1880, *"pidiendo el nombramiento de una comisión que redacte un mensaje a SS. MM. por haber preservado Dios sus vidas del atentado de que han sido objeto el 30 de diciembre de 1879* (II, 354). The final sentence bears the traditionalist stamp:

> "Nos hallaremos siempre unidos en todo lo que es hidalgo, todo lo que es español, todo lo que es grande" (II, 355).

When Doña Mercedes died in 1878, undoubtedly the most beloved queen of modern Spain, Campoamor showed that he shared in the general sorrow with a concise but effective quatrain:

> "¡Es un sueño de amor su triste historia!
> Nació, fué amable, candorosa y bella.
> Amó, reinó, murió, se abrió la gloria.
> Entró, y el cielo se cerró tras ella" (IV, 299).

These few verses were all that art really gained from Campoamor's devotion to three successive monarchs. In his *Poética* (1883), Campoamor went out of his way to make a flattering reference to Alfonso XII and his second wife (III, 299).

Despite this submissiveness, he had very definite opinions about the various public events and issues of his lifetime. We have already discussed his comments, contained in his *Historia crítica de las cortes reformadoras*, on the parliament which met in 1844 to reform the Constitution of 1837. A similar situation presented itself later, with the formation of the Unión Liberal.[7] Campoamor had by now developed into a stolid conservative; he took a reactionary stand in the matter, attacking in his *Polémicas con la democracia* (II, 384) this union of liberals and predicting that it would be part of the sad heritage which would be transmitted to Alfonso XII. These words suggest that Campoamor foresaw the upheaval of 1868. When the Revolution came, he condemned it as one of the foulest blots on Spanish history. He blamed above all Topete, who had brought shame upon the once-glorious Spanish fleet. Campoamor was pleased to be able to make a scapegoat of the

---

[7] *Vide* H. Butler Clarke, *Modern Spain* (Cambridge University Press, 1906), chap. xi.

admiral, for they had been bitter enemies since 1863, when they had vituperated each other from the columns of *La Epoca* and *El Contemporáneo* respectively and had finally fought a duel in which Topete was injured. The episode is related at length by Ildefonso Antonio Bermejo, the editor of *La Epoca*, in his work *La estafeta de palacio* (1872). The description is reproduced by Campoamor in his *Polémicas con la democracia* (2nd edit., II, 664ff.). Thus does Campoamor define the progressively more ignoble rôle of the Spanish navy in nineteenth-century politics:

"Vemos con escándalo y vergüenza que de sublevación en sublevación la parte mejor de aquella escuadra que acababa de sostener tan bizarramente la honra del pabellón nacional en una guerra, por cierto bastante injusta, contra algunas de las repúblicas de América de origen español,[8] vino por último a concluir por ser mandada en Cartagena por una cuadrilla de presidiarios que han reproducido en las costas de su misma patria las fechorías de los antiguos piratas argelinos."[9] (II, 662).

What of the cultural and philosophical history of the period? The most constant theme in Campoamor's comments is his hostility to the Krausist school. The outstanding characteristic of this group was *la seriedad*. As early as 1855, Campoamor declared his hatred of *la seriedad*, cultivated by D. Facundo Goñi, who had been imprudent enough to criticize the *Filosofía de las leyes*. The offended philosopher retorted in *El personalismo*:

"El señor Goñi es uno de esos escritores *serios* que creen que al público se le debe hablar siempre bajo la máscara de la gravedad. Yo aborrezco todos los disfraces, y el de la gravedad afectada me parece más risible que la ligereza sistemática" (I, 281).

Campoamor's enmity toward the Krausist school proper first revealed itself in his *Polémicas con la democracia*. He constantly accused Canalejas of being a Kantian and presumably a Krausist. To Castelar, who had described Krause as the last of the great spiritualist philosophers, he replied with an allusion to *"el vergonzante panteísmo del abstrusísimo Krause"* (II, 553).

Later, during the Restoration, Campoamor became involved in a polemic dealing directly with Krausism. The relevant documents have

[8]A reference to the inglorious war of 1865-66 with Peru and Chile and the "victory" of Callao (May 2, 1866).

[9]H. Butler Clarke (*ibid*, 342) gives an adequate description of the federalist rising in Cartagena (1873).

been collected and published in the *Obras completas*, III, under the title *Polémicas sobre el panenteísmo*. Campoamor provoked this disturbance of the peace with the prologue which he wrote for the book of poems *Dudas y tristezas* (1875) of Manuel de la Revilla.[10] Don Ramón bestowed the highest praise on poems written in his own epigrammatic manner, such as "El tren eterno":

—¡Alto el tren!—Parar no puede
—¿Ese tren a dónde va?
—Por el mundo caminando
    En busca del ideal.
—¿Cómo se llama?—Progreso
—¿Quién va en él?—La humanidad
—¿Quién le dirige?—Dios mismo
—¿Cuándo parará?—Jamás.

Campoamor nevertheless maintained that Revilla's whole thought was poisoned by his affiliations with the Krausist school. He supports this criticism with the following uncompromising dictum:

"De todos los sistemas filosóficos conocidos pueden salir artistas, poetas y escritores, menos del Krausismo" (II, 19).

He not unjustly accused Krause of stealing elements from many of the famous philosophers in order to construct his composite philosophy:

"Manufacturó su panenteísmo artificioso, robando a Espinosa la idea de substancia para llamarla *esencia*, a Descartes y a Fichte el método, a Schelling y a Hegel unas veces los medios y otras el fin" (III, 21).

The Krausist F. de P. Canalejas wrote a polite reply to Campoamor. He used urbane phrases to veil his indignation at the insults to his master, Sanz del Río, which were implicit in Campoamor's preface. With better feelings than style, Don Francisco wrote:

"En la escuela krausista me eduqué y tuve por dicha un maestro, cuya memoria venero, y no quiero que pase, sin desagraviar su respetable nombre, la airade página que usted escribe, y que cae

---

[10]Manuel de la Revilla y Moreno (1846-1881) became, in the following year (1876) professor of literature at the University of Madrid. His early death was due in part to overwork, but also to the nervous strain caused by the attacks of his critics, among whom must be numbered Campoamor. The Ateneo published, after his death, the *Obras de don Manuel de la Revilla* (1883), for which Cánovas del Castillo, whom Revilla criticizes in this polemic, wrote a eulogistic preface.

sobre la noble figura del que trajo a España y difundió entre nosotros las doctrinas de Krause" (III, 38).

Canalejas proceeded to describe the diversity of the Krausist movement which, he maintained, could not be considered as one and condemned *en bloc*:

"No hay ya escuela. Van unos a un teísmo racional y cristiano, propenden otros a un positivismo comedido y circunspecto; retroceden algunos, aguijoneados por la duda, a la Crítica de la Razón pura de Kant, tomando puerto y sagrado en ella, y esta diversidad de direcciones es muy propria del solícito afán con que el doctor Sanz del Río procuraba despertar en toda inteligencia el sello característico, original e individualísmo, que acompaña al hombre" (III, 38-39).

A few pages later, Canalejas counterblasted Campoamor's criticisms with an enthusiastic panegyric of Sanz del Río:

"No llevo con paciencia la desatención y la injuria al ilustre profesor, y es a todas luces injusto lo que sobre su capacidad y merecimientos se ha escrito por sus detractores. Enamorado de la ciencia, como nadie; indulgente y tolerante con las opiniones ajenas, como no se ha visto ejemplar en esta España, en que corre por nuestras venas sangre muslímica oxigenada por la inquisición; severo y metódico en el raciocinio, como el matemático más cumplido; vigoroso en el examen psicológico, de manera que comparados con él, parecen discreteos mujeriegos las observaciones de las escuelas escocesa y parisiense [!]; analítico, con una proligidad fecunda, que no había visto antes ni he vuelto a ver después; abundante en intuiciones; original y conocedor por larga meditación de los afanes de la filosofía novísima, Sanz del Río es superior a todos los filósofos españoles y franceses de este siglo y marcha a la par de Rosmini y Gioberti, los grandes pensadores de la Italia. No peca el juicio por encomiástico" (III, 40-41).

The last sentence is reassuring.

Campoamor wrote in reply a long and incoherent letter entitled "¡A la lenteja! ¡A la lenteja!," which contains only one remark which is to the point: namely, that Krausism must inevitably have political results.

Canalejas was justified in opening his next article with the following words:

"La réplica de usted no simplifica la controversia comenzada, antes al contrario, la extiende, pero desparramándola, gracias a incesantes explosiones de luces y de fuegos" (III, 63).

Canalejas deals with Campoamor's arguments one by one, constantly implying that the thought-content of his brilliant phrases was very small:

"Quedo esperando argumentos y razones que disculpen sus elocuentes filípicas de usted contra Krause y contra los krausistas" (III, 75).

Canalejas concluded his letter with a categorical defense of Krausism:
"Confesará siempre la crítica, que se debe al Krausismo el sentimiento de respeto a la filosofía, la convicción de que es preciso método y rigor en la indagación de la verdad, la seguridad de que el dato de conciencia ofrece luz y norte, y no pocas veces fundamento, la libertad para razonar sin mira concebida ni propósito interesado, la verdad de que en Dios está el principio de la ciencia y el noble empeño de que obremos, pensemos y queramos con conciencia de nuestros pensamientos y actos para no desear lo injusto y para huír del mal" (III, 83).

Meanwhile, poor Manuel de la Revilla, witnessing the bilious squabble to which his innocent book of poems had given rise, and the discourteous behaviour of Campoamor, became distressed and wrote a letter to Don Ramón, expressing approval of his ideas (since he himself had meanwhile abandoned the Krausist philosophy), but dismay at the unjudicial way in which they were expressed:

"No tengo para qué defender a la escuela krausista de los ataques que usted la dirige bajo el punto de vista metafísico . . . pero de esto a tratarla con la injusticia, con la intemperancia, con la intencionada saña que usted revela en su polémica, hay un abismo que yo no puedo, ni debo, ni quiero salvar" (III, 88).

Revilla repeated the reproach of Canalejas that the most reprehensible aspect of Campoamor's behaviour was its malicious inopportunity; he had seen fit to make his vicious attacks on the Krausists at a time when they were suffering persecution at the hands of Cánovas del Castillo and his ministry; he had even expressed unmitigated approval of this persecution:

"¡Ah, señor Campoamor! Cuando el adversario está indefenso, cuando la desgracia y la persecución le abruman, no es justo, ni caritativo denostarle, y menos excitar contra él las iras de la opinión y del poder. Esa polémica hubiera sido un acto de valentía, ya que no de buen gusto, cuando el Krausismo reinaba en las esferas officiales; hoy es un acto que yo no quiero calificar" (III, 90-91).

Campoamor retorted with a long reply (about fifty pages) entitled "Repito que ¡a la lenteja!" It is divided into two parts, the first addressed to Canalejas, the second to Revilla. Campoamor was particularly irritated with "*la destemplada ingerencia del señor Revilla*" (III, 94). Campoamor, who had introduced the crudely *ad hominem* tone into the polemic, had the effrontery to protest:

> "Los insultos no son razones. Me parece de una buena crianza un poco disputable, el que porque un escritor califique con más o menos dureza una doctrina, se le califique a él de *desagradecido* (¿de qué?), *sofista*, *díscolo*, etc., etc., y todo porque no entiende a Krause" (III, 94).

The reactionary who, in his earlier days, had treated the classical philosophers in a decidedly cavalier fashion, replied with childish petulance that he was unwilling to argue with anyone who failed to show them due respect:

> "A los que traten con soberano desdén a ingenios como Descartes, Espinosa y Kant, para deificar a un talento muy mediano, no les daré yo el gusto de discutir con ellos en tono apocalíptico, para ocuparme en cosas enredadas, *sin gracia* y *sin sentido*" (III, 97).

He was offended by Canalejas' harsh but apt remark that he was writing for "*las tenderas conservadoras.*" He refused to retract his approval of the persecution of the Krausists by the Cánovas ministry:

> "Le repito al señor Canalejas que es una prueba de *muy buen gusto* en el ministerio Cánovas el procurar saber si en las Universidades se quiere convertir en *ciencia* lo que en la calle es motín" (III, 123).

This remark bears very clearly the hall-mark of reaction. Indeed, a passing observation of Campoamor suggests that his hatred of Krause was motivated by the fundamental socialism of the German:

> "Resume toda su política estableciendo el Comunismo. Ahora pregunto yo, a mi vez: ¿Concibe el señor Revilla que se puede encerrar al género humano en el falansterio de la Comunidad?" (III, 135).

Canalejas was disgusted at Campoamor's lack of delicacy. He said his last word in an article entitled "Fin de polémica," in which he stressed the simple fact that, whatever the theoretical considerations might be, three noble men, namely Salmerón, Giner, and Azcárate had lost their chairs and were suffering persecution:

> "¡El día en que se conoció ese fallo fué día tristísimo para la enseñanza universitaria! ¡Es un día negro para la ciencia! No hablo

movido por amistad, sino por severa justicia. Los tres son irrem-
plazables; los tres figuraban en primera línea y en los primeros puestos
en el profesorado en España. El señor Salmerón es la inteligencia
más profunda, más perspicua, de mayor aliento de cuantas poblaban
nuestros claustros. Su elocuencia didáctica no tiene rival ni seme-
jante. Es una gloria nacional. Giner de los Ríos es un devoto de
la ciencia, noble, entusiasta; mayor pureza y elevación de miras en
el estudio no las conozco. Su religiosidad científica, su amor al
estudio, su desprecio a todo otro interés o propósito, avasalla y en-
amora a cuantos le escuchan. Su instrucción es tan vasta como
precisa, enérgica y elegante su palabra. Azcárate es un espíritu dulce
y reflexivo, tolerante y discreto, cuyos progresos se notaban, no de
día en día, sino de hora en hora" (III, 145-46).

Azcárate was apparently like those exotic plants whose growth can be
perceived with the naked eye.

Revilla likewise showed his unwillingness to argue in a brief article
entitled "Ultima palabra." The quarrel of which he had been the
innocent cause was apparently poisoning his life. In order to free himself from all responsibility, he affirms in italics:

"*Yo no tuve conocimiento a su debido tiempo del prólogo de mis
poesías*" (III, 153).

Juan Sieiro,[11] who seems to have been much interested in the subject
under discussion but intimidated by the ugliness of the quarrel, wrote to
Campoamor a letter dated August 4, 1875, in which he expressed his
opinions on the relationship between pantheism and dualism. He concluded ironically with a request not to be dragged into a public controversy:

"Termino rogándole que por ningún concepto dé publicidad a mi
escrito y sobre todo *a mi persona*" (III, 158).

Campoamor was in no mood to pay attention to etiquette, so he scotched
Juan Sieiro in a somewhat abusive letter dated August 17, 1875.

Rafael Montoro,[12] who had followed the polemic with interest,
published an article entitled "El panenteísmo" in the *Revista Europea*,

---

[11]Juan Sieiro González (1835-1893), a Galician pedagogue and a Krausist philosopher;
he published a number of general philosophical works.

[12]Rafael Montoro (1852-1933), a Cuban literary critic, who resided for many years in
Madrid and was a prominent figure at the Ateneo. He published in *El Norte* and in
El Tiempo criticisms of several of Campoamor's works. After '98, he was prominent
in Cuban politics.

No. 77, praising Canalejas and condemning Campoamor for his lack of generosity. Don Ramón continued to show this characteristic in his reply, in which he said resentfully:

"Me dicen que Krause ha sido modesto, sincero, laborioso, honrado, pobre y perseguido, añadiendo: '¿habrá quien no sienta que se le oprima el corazón cuando le hablan en términos destemplados e injustos de esa severa y pura moral, noblemente enseñada con la palabra y el ejemplo?' " (III, 166).

Campoamor was implying that his rivals were trying to play upon his feelings. This was decidedly unjust, for Campoamor was relentlessly insulting a group of men in whom posterity has recognized at least one outstanding virtue: a high moral sense and a quixotic scrupulousness.

This letter of Campoamor marked the end of the polemic proper. Six years later, Manuel de la Revilla published another edition of his poems. The prologue, either by its republication or by its omission, would reawaken slumbering hatreds. Revilla adopted the middle course of asking Campoamor, in a letter dated January 25, 1881, to revise his prologue, suppressing the references to Krausism. He complained of the misfortunes which the now historic quarrel had brought upon him. He had squabbled with González Serrano so grievously that their friendship had been broken. In order not to provoke petulant Campoamor, Revilla attributed all the trouble to *"la feroz intolerancia de los krausistas"* (III, 171-72). Admittedly Revilla had abandoned his Krausist beliefs, but he loses some of our esteem by thus flattering the vanity of a petty old gentleman. Be that as it may, the poet complied and revised his prologue (III, 175-184).

CHAPTER XVI

THE THEORIST IN PRACTICE

THE active rôle of Campoamor in Spanish politics is now almost forgotten. Soon after the publication of his *Filosofía de las leyes*, he suddenly rose to political power; toward the end of 1847, he was appointed governor of the province of Castellón de la Plana by Luis José Sartorius, later Conde de San Luis. The poet-politician relates whimsically in *El personalismo*:

"Instalado en mi ínsula, quise, como Sancho, ser justo y promover el bien. ¡Inexperto! No sabía yo que para hacer, mandando, estas dos cosas tan difíciles era menester empezar por respetar los *trámites*" (I, 339).

He proceeds to pen a pointed satire of the hindrance created by the endless *trámites* of Spanish administration. Like his flippant attitude toward the hide-bound Academia Española, his disgust with *la tramitología* won him many sympathies. The story circulated that, the first time an *expediente* was brought to him, he apostrophized the bearer with these words:

"¿Les parece a ustedes que me paga el Gobierno para que pierda el tiempo leyendo estas tonterías que ustedes han escrito para pasarlo?"[1]

Campoamor showed, but in vain, a more constructive attitude in the question of education. As he relates cynically in *El personalismo*:

"En mi entusiasmo de hacer a mis subordinados felices a la fuerza, dispuse, o, por mejor decir, decreté que la instrucción primera fuese *obligatoria*, medida que llevé a cabo con un ardor digno de que me apoyase la ilustración del Gobierno, como efectivamente no me apoyó" (I, 340).

The government must nonetheless have been satisfied with Campoamor's administration, for, a year later, Roca de Togores, first Marqués de Molins, appointed him governor of the province of Alicante. Campoamor, disillusioned as a reformer, had determined to enjoy a burocratic *dolce far niente*. But the sacred fire refused to be extinguished. As he tells us in *El personalismo*:

"Yo en mi segundo mando ma había propuesto imitar en parte a esa raza de gobernantes morosos, tacaños y modestos, para quienes

---

[1] *Vide* González-Blanco, *op. cit.*, 195.

la felicidad pública consiste en su comodidad privada. Pero ¡ay!. los caracteres decididos somos como la gata en visita: apenas pasa el ratón de la circunstancia damos al traste con todas nuestras pre-determinaciones. Así es que poco a poco fuí introduciendo todas cuantas reformas me habían atraído disgustos en mi primer período gubernamental, y sólo con respecto a instrucción primaria no me atreví a llevar adelante mi sistema socialista de hacerla obligatoria, pues ví pronto que en aquella provincia hay hartas gentes dispuestas a volver por sus fueros y de seguro muchos padres me hubieran probado que ellos tenían el imprescindible derecho de consentir que sus hijos fuesen unos burros" (I, 312).

If Campoamor achieved few or no positive results as governor of Alicante, he at least overcame a catastrophe which almost brought desolation to his province. Between 1849 and 1851, plague spread across the Mediterranean and threatened to invade Spain, an eventuality which the Duke of Valencia and his ministry sought to stave off. The situation was especially critical at Alicante, whence twenty thousand people emigrated yearly to Algiers, now the centre of infection. The government therefore ordered Campoamor to suspend emigration, but failed to provide him with the money necessary to allay the misery caused by this act:

"Disponiendo sólo de los medios ordinarios y sin faltar a una sola prescripción legal, logramos por espacio de mucho tiempo entretener en obras públicas a mas de 2,000 trabajadores diarios, aliviando la miseria de tantos infelices como hubieran sido arrastrados al sepulcro o al destierro" (I, 343).

Campoamor concludes this autobiographical passage from El personalismo with a naïve boast:

"Este acto de caridad y de alta política . . . honrará siempre nuestro corazón y nuestra inteligencia" (I, 344).

The Madrid government apparently was pleased with Campoamor's handling of the crisis, for he was shortly afterwards appointed governor of Valencia by the ministry of Egaña. Campoamor fell in love with the Levantine province he now controlled:

"En aquel país . . . todo es encantador, todo es risueño" (I, 345).

Once more, Campoamor does not hesitate to inform us of his brilliancy as an administrator and as a reformer:

"Mis inteligentes secretarios, los señores don Joaquín Ferreres y don José Palarea, saben con cuánto desvelo y tolerancia hemos gobernado juntos por espacio de mucho tiempo. Apelo a su espíritu de alta imparcialidad para que digan si mi gobierno no ha sido la realización práctica de mis principios teóricos, si mi mando no ha sido un *curso de personalismo*" (I, 346).

This ingenuous appeal to the "high impartiality" of his co-administrators suggests that Campoamor had been subjected to criticism which still rankled.

The poet's career as provincial governor was cut short by the Revolution of 1854. Remembering that one of his predecessors at Valencia, Miguel Antonio Camacho, had been assassinated in the 1843 uprising, Campoamor feared for his life. A feeling of shameful horror came over him whenever he recalled the tense moment when the revolutionary mob approached his palace:

"Jamás me acuerdo sin rubor de haberme visto inerme y a la merced de una muchedumbre insureccionada" (I, 349).

Fortunately, the crowd, instead of assassinating him, carried him in triumph through the streets, thus endearing Valencia forever to his heart.

However, Campoamor lost his job as a result of the revolution, and it was doubtless this in part which made him a most bitter critic of the event and of its instigators, the Army. The revolution came:

"seguida, como casi siempre, de todas las plagas de Egipto, la peste, le guerra, el hambre y una plaga de difamadores que podremos llamar los *animales inmundos*. ¡Ah! se me había olvidado citar entre las plagas revolucionarias el asesinato y el incendio. Recuerdo con este motivo que, pasando entonces por una de las capitales de Andalucía, leí un boletín oficial que decía: 'A la hora de la salida del correo, el pueblo de Madrid estaba incendiando las casas de tal y tal y tal. ... Lo que se anuncia al público *para su satisfacción*.' Al considerar estas satisfacciones de los demagogos españoles ¿no es verdad que parecen atenienses los moros del Riff? No es cierto que aquella expresión que en pleno Parlamento nos regaló cierto representante francés de que 'el Africa empieza en los Pirineos' da gana concluírla de este modo 'y acaba en las columnas de Hércules'? (I, 347).

In these remarks, the Francophile partisan of *europeización* in seen strangely mingled with the budding reactionary.

Campoamor concludes the description of his attempts, as provincial governor, to cultivate the garden entrusted to him, with a melodramatic passage which, being on the whole serious, amuses but fails to impress:

"Si algún día, como no es imposible, por zaherir, como Socrates, a la democracia y por repeler del gobierno a los ignorantes y a los ineptos, me veo obligado a apurar la cicuta, yo, que me siento, aunque algunos afectan que no lo creen, con alguna virtud más y algún defectillo menos de los que communmente se estilan, en vez de someterme a ninguna de las tontolatrías con que de vez en cuando la humanidad se embrutece, apuraré impasible la pócima decretada.

Entonces mi cuerpo se elevará a la categoría de reliquia, y, en el caso fortuita de esta deificación futura, lego mis mortales, y entonces inmortales restos a la ciudad de Valencia. En agradecimiento a su cariño, la consagro en muerte mi cuerpo, así como en vida mi alma" (I, 350).

After 1854, Campoamor did not disappear from the political scene. On the contrary, as a conservative deputy, he took a prominent part in the political discussions of the capital. At first his conservatism was liberal; thus it was, as already related, that he attacked the proposals to restrict the freedom of the press, especially in his speech of July 4, 1857, condemning the obscurantist law sponsored by Nocedal and González Bravo. As the years passed, Campoamor became more and more conservative in his parliamentary attitude. This development can be traced through his speeches, the most important of which are to be found in Volume II of his *Obras completas*.

Don Ramón rose to modest fame in the parliamentary hierarchy. For many years, he was a member of the Consejo de Estado, but his participation in the discussions was so light-hearted that, on one occasion, the president, Ríos Rosas, was obliged to interrupt him with the comment:

"El Sr. Campoamor, en vez de ilustrar las cuestiones, las ameniza."[2] The poet later became Director General de Beneficencia y de Sanidad, but he had by this time degenerated into a diehard without imagination and without initiative, and he left no trace in an office so rich in potentialities.

---

[2] *Vide* González Blanco, *op. cit.*, 195-96.

CHAPTER XVII

INTERNATIONAL RELATIONS, IMPERIALISM

CAMPOAMOR'S attitude toward imperialism, both of the past and of his own time, was a direct outcome of his general ethnic philosophy. He regarded the white race as the pre-ordained protector of the yellow, copper-colored, and black peoples. A further distinction is necessary. Of the two almost antithetical branches of the Caucasian half of the white race, Campoamor maintained the southern group to show conspicuous incapacity in its violent attempts at colonization, in striking contrast with the northern group which, Campoamor tells us, displays cool tenacity in its well-planned efforts: The Spaniard asserts in *El personalismo*:

"Estos [los pueblos meridionales] son demasiado ardorosos para dejar de ser conquistadores, son demasiado ligeros para ser buenos conquistadores. Los pueblos del Norte, pour el contrario, tienen harta frialdad para tomar inciativas temerarias y demasiada rectitud y prepotencia para no regularizar las escilaciones extremadas" (I, 88).

Campoamor regarded the great Roman Empire as the first monster engendered by meridional imperialism. He praises the Teutons for having broken the yoke of Rome, but his eulogy is full of implicit contradictions:

"Los teutones, demasiadamente constreñidos hacia sus estériles regiones por las tiránicas usurpaciones de Roma, estimulados par las invasiones tártaro-escíticas, se abrieron paso con la espada, volcando para siempre al más duro avasallador de la especie humana" (I, 88).

This was but a Pyrrhic victory, for the southern oppressor grew once more, this time in the form of the medieval church. Again the Germans destroyed the Roman tyranny, thus winning Campoamor's loud approval:

"Los alemanes, a la voz de Lutero, rebelados contra las usurpaciones espirituales y la codicia del más caballeresco y más culto de los Papas, establecieron la libertad religiosa, proclamando el libre examen y trasladando a la razón humana la supremacía que se habían arrogado los Supremos Pontífices" (I, 88).

Phoenix-like, the southern monster arose anew, now in Spain. Folowing the tradition of the *leyenda negra*, Compoamor in his liberal period damned the Spanish Empire with a vigor strengthened by his anti-clerical convictions. As an example of the nefarious activities of this theocratic empire, Campoamor quotes the biblioclasm committed by Texcoco by the first bishop of Mexico, the Franciscan Zumárraga. After describing the event, Campoamor concludes:

"Este maldecido obispo cometió una barbaridad tan inútil para la moral como perniciosa para la cultura humana" (I, 80).[1]

While Campoamor believed in the natural superiority of the white race and in the validity of its imperialistic rôle in history, the eighteenth-century tradition was still strong enough in him to lead him to condemn the usurpation of land and the destruction of life, although he fails to coordinate his views in this matter. Accepting uncritically the testimony of Las Casas, he accuses Spain of having set the world a bad example:

"Por desgracia, de cuarenta millones de hombres que pueblan la América, sólo ya la cuarta parte desciende de la raza indígena. ¡Tanta prisa nos hemos dado a usurparles la patria y a quitarles la vida! El padre Las Casas, tan buen cristiano como mal español, ha dejado al mundo una irrecusable y para nosotros ignominiosa prueba de quienes han sido los primeros que dieron el pernicioso ejemplo de tanta rapiña y de tanto asesinato" (I, 81).

This time, the offender was his own country, Spain, and the agent of Nemesis that traditional enemy, Great Britain. Campoamor was never sufficiently anti-traditionalist to carry his argument to its logical conclusion and to praise England wholeheartedly for its victory over Spain. He attempted to do so, but the words stuck in his throat:

Los isleños de la Gran Bretaña, después de proclamar el liberal principio de que 'los mares son de todos los pueblos,' resumiendo en su carácter nacional las cualidades más dominates de la rama caucasiana septentrional, con una insistencia silenciosa, flemática, arrogante, tradicional, han plantado su pabellón an las bocas de todos los Estrechos, se han apoderado de todas las islas estratégicamente esparcidas por el globo, y después de tener un arsenal en cada campo de batalla, se disponen a sostener sus derechos al dominio universal. Con esta política extensa, enérgica e invariable, la aristocrática Inglaterra ha sometido el mundo a un indigno pupilaje, y el orgulloso pedagogo, en sus aspiraciones de curador general, cuando alguno de sus edu-

---

[1] A discussion of the truth of this commonplace story is to be found in Joaquín García Icazbalceta, "La destrucción de antigüedades mexicanas atribuida a los misioneros en general y particularmente al Illmo. Sr. D. Fr. Juan de Zumárraga, primer obispo y Arzobispo de Mexico," *Obras* (Mexico: Victoriano Agueros, 1896), II, 5ff.

candos se rebela a sus consejos, le hace someterse por la fuerza de
las armas o por los halagos de la seducción. ¡Cuánto poder! ¡Cuánta
astucia!" (I, 89).

Canto XVI, entitled "Juicio del mundo," of the epic poem *Colón*
(1853), contains a judgment of the nations of the world by Faith, Hope,
and Charity.   The strophe referring to England (xxxviii) reveals admiration mingled with hatred:

"Pueblo heroico sin fin, de héroes no honrado,
Atanas espartana, Albion sombría
rey-pueblo, en cuya historia han encarnado
cien verdugos su vil genealogía,
témpano desde el polo desgajado
para aplastar al débil Mediodía,
plaza que el mar defiende y que bloquea
de exterminio y de luz futura tea. . ."

These artificial antitheses, and the apposition *"rey pueblo,"* show very
clearly the influence of Victor Hugo.

Later, in his reactionary period, Campoamor adopted the naïve traditionalist view of the Spanish Empire, while his latent hatred of the
British Empire burst noisily into the open.   He declaims in *El ideísmo:*

"El imperio español, la más desinteresada, la más noble, la más grande
y la más ideal de las dominaciones de la tierra, tuvo entonces héroes
como Gonzalo de Córdoba, Pizarro y Cortés, y aquel Vasco Núñez
de Balboa que tomó posesión del mar Pacífico metiéndose en el agua
hasta la cintura con un Cristo en la mano y en la otra la espada. Ante
estas maravillas de abnegación y de osadía, Alejandro parece un bus-
carruidos, César un facciose y Napoleón un revolucionario aprove-
chado.   Ved a los ingleses, con almas romanas y cuerpos de carta-
gineses, conquistando la India en nombre de una sociedad de comer-
ciantes y echando con astucia la zancadilla a todas las islas estraté-
gicas del globo para poder contrabandear, y notaréis la diferencia que
hay entre estos valientes pagados y aquellos héroes que dejan atrás
en idealismo y desinterés a todos los tipos de la andante caballería"
(III, 514-15).

Although, during his liberal years, he condemned as cruel and incom-
petent all Mediterranean imperialisms, including that of his own country,
Campoamor was never a defeatist or even a pacifist.   He might have been
described as a militant Pan-Iberian: he thought that Spain would never
accomplish its natural destiny until Castile had conquered Portugal,

Gibraltar, and the coast of Morocco.   He warns his fellow-countrymen in the *Historia crítica de las cortes reformadoras*:

"España debe tener siempre la vista clavada en Portugal, Gibraltar y el litoral de Marruecos; mientras ne se ize su pabellón en estos puntos, la nación sera siempre una banasta sin fondo" (II, 79).

The African policy of Spain must be:

"Vengar un resentimiento de muchos siglos, resentimiento que aun vive y que vivirá eternamente, mientras tengan sangre en las venas los descendientes del infeliz monarca que sucumbió en los campos de Jérez" (II, 80).

Campoamor evidently does not believe in letting bygones be bygones. In 1844, the assassination of a Spanish consul in Morocco created a grave situation.[2]   Martínez de la Rosa accepted the mediation of Great Britain, much to the disgust of Campoamor, who hoped that Spain would take this opportunity of rushing headlong into glory.   Although he loved French culture, he regarded French expansion in Africa as a danger which Spain should oppose to the limit.   Here again, he reproached Martínez de la Rosa for his moderation.

Spain has not yet forgotten the Armada and still nourishes a secret desire to become once more a great sea-power.   Even when he condemned Spain's former imperialism, Campoamor cherished this hope.   The failure of Armero[3] to rebuild the Spanish fleet aroused the poet's wrath.   He denounced this minister of the marine in a vitriolic passage of the *Historia crítica de las cortes reformadoras*:

"Si el señor Armero piensa que es ser buen Ministro de Marina el comprar media libra de brea con la cual se puede ensuciar la quilla de una falúa y el agenciar tres varas de lona para remendar un foque, le creo bastante pundonoroso para tomarme la libertad de aconsejarle que renuncie su sueldo de seis mil duros, porque podemos buscar un calafate que desempeñará su encargo mejor que él, por seis reales diarios" (II, 88-89).

In later years, the state of the Spanish navy improved considerably, thanks to the ministry of the Marqués de Molins, one of Campoamor's protectors.   After the already described journey on the newly-built rail-

---

[2]The assassination of the French-Jewish business man, M. Victor Darmon, who was also a consular agent for Spain, is related by Jerónimo Bécker, *Historia de Marruecos* (Madrid: Jaime Ratés, 1915), 206 ff.

[3]Francisco Armero y Peñaranda, Marqués de Nervión (1804-1867) was several times minister of the marine.

road from Madrid to Alicante, Isabel II sailed to Valencia in the reorganized and rejuvenated fleet.   She travelled aboard the warship "Francisco de Asís," while Campoamor was assigned to the "Perla."   He comments, in *Polémicas con la democracia*:

> "Al ver este germen de nuestro futuro poderío naval, no puedo menos de dirigir mis ojos hacia la quinta de mi amigo el marqués de Molins... al contemplar la mayor parte de los buques de la escuadra, de cuya construcción ha sido el autor, debe haber hallado una granda felicidad presenciando estos gloriosos resultados de su antigue poder" (II, 645).

It was Campoamor's cult of the erstwhile sea-power of Spain which led him to compose the epic *Colón* (1853).   In the best traditionalist vein, Campoamor depicts Columbus as a man of deep piety.   Canto III ("El Cielo") opens with an invocation which begins:

> "¡Ayudadme en mi empresa sobrehumana
> peregrinas virtudes teologales!
> ¡Guiadme, FE, lumbrera soberana
> que obscurecéis las luces eternales!
> ¡Valedme, CARIDAD, graciable hermana
> del más mísero y vil de los mortales!
> ¡Alentadme, ESPERANZA bendecida,
> último aliento de la humana vida!" (IV, 402).

At this pious request, the gates of Heaven open, and the three Virtues address Columbus at length.

The natural consequence of this cult of Spanish sea-power, and of this desire to see it reborn, should be an imperialistic interest in Latin America, both in the past and in the present.   As we have seen, it was not until late in his life that Campoamor began to cast a conqueror's eye on the New World.   For many years, he was indifferent, so that there was a contradiction between his cult of Spanish naval power and his hostility to the old trans-Atlantic imperialism.   He regarded Hispanic America with scorn.   Whereas Pardo-Bazán invoked Gumplovicz to prove that the races of Latin America have been strengthened by amalgamation, Campoamor, following his racial philosophy to its logical conclusion, considered them to be the mediocre products of a superior race with an inferior one.   He comments, in *El personalismo*:

> "Si la raza es mediocre, se forman entonces repúblicas inconsistentes, como casi todos los Estados de América de origen español, en los cuales un hombre superior los absorbe y tiraniza, ya llamándose presidente, como Rosas, ya titulándose emperador, como Bolívar" (I, 141-42).

From intercourse with such peoples no good can come, thought Campoamor, and he shunned the "hands-across-the-sea" attitude of neo-imperialists such as Pardo-Bazan:

> "En cambio de la esclavitud y del mal gobierno que las repúblicas de América han heredado de su antigua metrópoli, nos han regalado dos plagas más mortíferas mil veces que el mal gobierno y la esclavitud: una enfermedad, que ruboriza el nombrarla, y las rebeliones o pronunciamientos militares" (I, 347).

Traditionalist Spaniards in the last century were unwilling to accept the independence of the former Spanish colonies as irrevocable, and many were the schemes to plant Spain's banner once more in the soil of the New World.   Mexico was thought by one section of these retro-imperialists to offer the best chances for some putsch.   It was with this in mind that the Marqués de Pidal and his ministry proposed to obtain satisfaction for supposed insults which the Mexican republic had inflicted on Spain.   Campoamor expressed his opposition to any such attempt in a speech which he made on May 26, 1857.

This address is in striking contrast with another which Campoamor made in the Cortes eight years later, on February 17, 1865, in which he voiced his indignation at the proposal of the government to abandon Santo Domingo.   Evidently demanding military action, he cried:

> "Si yo fuera compañero del señor Gándara,[4] preferiría mil veces morir en el campo de batalla que venir a España a morirme de vergüenza. No sé yo por dónde van a venir esos 20,000 hombres, que creo que son 20,000 los que hay allí.   ¿Van a venir por el mismo camino que llevaron los 600 compañeros de Hernán Cortés, que ellos solos conquistaron todo el Imperio de Méjico?" (II, 349-350).

This last rheotorical question is topographically grotesque.   Be that as it may, the appeal to Hernán Cortés clearly shows Campoamor's development into a retro-imperialist.   Although his ultimate position was naïve and unrealistic, he had at least coordinated his attitudes toward America and toward Spain's naval power.

---

[4]General José de la Gándara y Navarro (1820-1885) was responsible both for the proposal and for the carrying out of the evacuation of Santo Domingo   He has left a work entitled *Anexión y guerra de Santo Domingo*.

CHAPTER XVIII

International Relations. Diplomacy

In his *Filosofía de las leyes*, Campoamor on one point declared his open disagreement with his master Montesquieu: he refused to accept the *philosophe's* view that peace is "natural" (II, 267-68).[1]

Yet Campoamor did not believe in the rule of force. He held that the abuse of warpower is avenged by nemesis, and that, in the end, only just wars are successful:

> "Aun en estado de guerra, jamás se cometen impunemente las transgresiones de la moral. Cuando un pueblo provoca una guerra injusta, tarde o temprano recibe el castigo de su immoralidad, ya pasando por la ignominia de ser vencido, ya si es vencedor, sufriendo los remordimientos que continuamente despierta en su corazón el Dios más justo y más inexorable de la tierra, la conciencia de la humanidad" (II, 269).

These last phrases are in the best eighteenth-century style. The trust in historical justice is consoling.

In diplomacy Campoamor never had any faith. All its varied forms seemed to him equally deserving of condemnation as a trickster's art: He says in *El personalismo:*

> "Las intrigas políticas y comerciales de una nación están en razón directa del número de sus agentes diplomáticos.
>
> La Turquía es la nación europea de más moralidad internacional, porque recibe embajadores y no los envía. Con esta cauta nación se va a efectuar la fábula del labrador y la culebra.
>
> La diplomacia es tan rica en géneros como la literatura: la hay vanidosa como la de los griegos, que tenían a mucha honra ganarse la aquiescencia de las demás naciones: soberbia como la romana, que delegaba a los reyes extranjeros el poder de juzgar en sus mismos dominios; infame como la del consejo de Venecia, que se libraba de sus enemigos con el puñal o con el veneno; subrepticia o ergotista como la de los papas, suspicaz y petulante como la española, verbosa y galante como la francesa, corruptora e inteligente como la inglesa y modesta y mercachiflera como la norteamericana" (I, 215).

The only remedy for the evils of diplomacy was, according to the liberal Campoamor of the *Filosofía de las leyes*, the abolition of its

---

[1] "La paix serait la première loi naturelle"—Montesquieu, *Esprit des lois*, Book I, chap. ii.

secrecy and of its bilateral character, and the establishment of a public and general diplomatic court, what would now be called the League of Nations:

"Si hay autoridades que rijan la asociación municipal, la provincial y la nacional, ignoro por qué motivo no ha de haber un congreso general permanente que establezca principios y que dirima todas las contiendas de la asociación universal. Un hombre podía ser un hijo de tal pueblo, individuo de cual nación, y llamarse al mismo tiempo ciudadano del universo. . . . La razón y el interés recíproco reclaman imperiosamente una asociación universal" (II, 270-71).

During his reactionary period, and following the usual reactionary pattern, Campoamor attempted to ridicule the ideas of internationalism and cosmopolitanism which he had previously advocated. He subjected to his satire not only the political aspect of this ideal, but also the linguistic problem, the creation of a universal language such as Esperanto. In his *Discurso en la Real Academia Española*, he said scornfully:

"¿Cuál utopia es la más irrealizable, la lengua universal o la paz universal? Cada una de estas quimeras tiene sus maniáticos generosos. Pero las idólatras de la lengua universal son más en número y más propagandistas" (I, 390).

The War of 1870 damped Campoamor's bellicose ardor and convinced him of the uselessness of war. In the *"dolora dramática" Guerra a la guerra*, which was played with great success at the Teatro Español on November 3, 1870, Campoamor depicts a bloody battlefield on which two soldiers, the one French, the other German, meet and converse at great length (in Spanish, of course!). Although sincere patriots, they feel that they are fighting for vain causes:

Enrique: Soy alemán.
Victor: Soy francés. ¿Estaréis de gozo llenos?
Enrique: Si, tenemos la unidad.
Victor: Y eso, ¿os dará libertad?
Enrique: Libertad, no.
Victor: ¿y manos?
Enrique: ¡Menos! [Enrique has lost his hands].
Victor: Pues ¿qué has ganado?
Enrique: Soy franco, lo que he ganado aún no sé" (VI, 21-22).

This duet closes with an appeal to Christ that he put an end to war. Victor, with hands crossed, prays:

"¡Venga a nosotros, Señor,

aquel que a este mundo trajo
la justicia y el trabajo,
la fe, la paz y el amor!
¡Héroe humilde de Belén
purga de monstruos la tierra
y líbranos de la guerra
por siempre jamás!
Enrique: ¡Amén! (VI, 36).

As for international trade, Campoamor was, during his liberal period and clearly under English influence, a convinced free-trader. In the *Filosofía de las leyes*, he formulates thus his basic economic principle:

"No se hace, o no se debe hacer una cosa mala y costosa, cuando por una permuta se la puede adquirir buena y barata" (II, 274).

Campoamor later applies this theory implicitly to Spain:

"Si vuestro país produce exclusivamente exquisitos limones y naranjas, no debéis dedicaros más que a perfeccionar vuestras naranjas y
vuestros limones. El que quiera probar vuestras naranjas tendrá
que cederos en cambio los preciosos artefactos de sus manufacturas.
Quien desee gustar vuestros limones se verá precisado a trocarlos
por otros deliciosos frutos de su industria rural" (id.).

It would follow then that Campoamor opposed the industrialization of Spain which many liberals, such as Ortega y Gasset, have advocated, and likewise the building, at the instigation of Catalan industrialists, of high tariff-walls around the Peninsula.

In the normal course of events, Campoamor would, in his develop-ment toward reaction, have rejected the free-trade ideas of his youth. However, this development was thwarted because, as J. B. Guardiola declared in an article, published in *La Razón*, which offended Campoamor, the Spanish democrats decided in favor of protection, while the con-servatives, such as D. Pedro Egaña and the Conde de San Luis, and the conservative newspapers *La España* and *El Heraldo*, advocated a modi-fied form of free-trade. Campoamor explains this matter at length in his *Polémicas con la democracia* (II, 392ff.). He reveals a certain in-consistency in attacking the democrat Castelar for going to the other extreme of recommending complete free-trade. In his reactionary period, Campoamor seems to have seen democrats to the right of him, democrats to the left of him, democrats all round him. However, his attachment to the general principle of free-trade is one of the few beliefs which, for admittedly unusual reasons, Campoamor did not reverse in the course of the years.

CONCLUSION

Disregarding the general contempt in which Campoamor, especially Campoamor the prose-writer, is held, we have shown that his utterly neglected prose-works constitute a highly valuable document for the intellectual life of nineteenth century Spain; that he was surprisingly well-read; that, despite everything, his ideas were built upon a solid and ample framework; that, in applying these ideas to the world around him, he showed an unrequited love of consistency; that he incidentally made some startling and tragic prophecies; in brief, that the subject of this study, which at first sight might seem insignificant and pointless, is in reality of definite interest.

Our task has been complicated by the radical development in Campoamor's ideas, as explained in the first chapter. We have seen that the Campoamor of the middle, liberal period was usually in direct contradiction with the early traditionalist and the late reactionary. Without committing ourselves as to the objective validity of these opposing attitudes, we should find it very difficult to deny that from the viewpoint of intellectual interest and historical significance, the middle period far outshadows its neighbours. No reproach can therefore be directed at us for devoting to it most of our attention.

INDEX

Academia Española, 6, 9, 17-18, 22, 45, 92, 99, 106, 130.
Academia de la Historia, 66-67.
Acevedo, José, 23.
Adamson, Robert, 27.
Adelanto, El, 60.
Agost, 64.
Alas, Leopoldo, 98, 111.
Alcazarquivir, 78.
Alexander, 65, 136.
Alexander VI, Pope, 83.
Alexandria, 78.
Alfaric, Prosper, 15.
Alfonso XII, 45, 121-122.
Algiers, 131.
Alicante, 6-7, 29, 32, 63-64, 130-131, 138.
Alvarez de Lorenzana, Juan, 10.
Alzugaray, Ricardo, 10.
Ammon, 69.
Anacreon, 41.
Anaxagoras, 104.
Andalusia, 18, 132.
Anglo-Saxons, 108-113.
Annamese, 76.
Año Político, El, 24.
Antón del Olmet, Luis and García Carraffa, Arturo, 67.
Antón y Ferrándiz, Manuel, 69.
Apollo, 81, 104.
Arabs, 71, 77-79, 116, 132.
Aragon, 96, 118.
Aranda, 120.
Araucanians, 73.
Arbodeya Martínez, Maximiliano, 37.
Archimedes, 65, 87.
Aristotle, 35, 106, 111.
Armero y Peñaranda, Francisco, 137.
Asturias, 3-4, 16, 18, 82.
Ateneo de Madrid, 10, 21-22, 24, 43, 46, 124.
Athens, 60, 82.
Attila, 63.
Auñón, Marqués de, 45.
Australians, 68.
Austro-Hungary, 106.
Auvergne, Edmund B. d', 121.
Avanzadi, Telesforo de, 68.
Azcárate, 127-128.

Bacon, 25, 111.
Baillie, H. B., 7.
Balart, Federico, 10.
Balboa, Vasco Núñez de, 136.
Balmes, Jaime, 30, 37, 84.
Balzac, Honoré de, 96-97.
Barca Corral, Francisco, 10.
Barcelona, 96.
Bastemeti, 60.
Bauer, Bruno, 105.
Beausobre, 15.
Beccaria, 51.
Bécker, Jerónimo, 137.
Bécquer, 43.
Bengoechea, Alejandro de, 13.
Benito de Endara, Lorenzo, 24.
Benoît, Pierre, 112.
Bentham, 51.
Bermejo, Ildefonso, 6, 123.
Bernard, Claude, 15, 22.
Berzosa, Antonio, 10.
Biblioteca Nacional, 5.
Bismarck, 107.
Blumenbach, 69.
Boada y Balmes, Miguel, 10.
Bolívar, 138.
Bordas-Demoulin, 94.
Bosanquet, Bernard, 20.
Bossuet, 66, 91.
Boucke, O. Fred, 16.
British Empire. *See* England.
Broca, 69.
Browning, Robert, 27, 60.
Brunetière, 14.
Bryan, J. Ingram, 76.
Buchanan, David, 16.
Büchner, Ludwig, 22.
Buffon, 14.
Bulgars, 74.
Burgos, 93.
Burmese, 76.
Burrell, Julio, 24.
Bury, J. B., 70.
Busquet, G. H., 16.

Cabanis, Pierre-Jean-Georges, 19.
Cæsar, 88, 136.
Calderón de la Barca, 41, 83, 119.

Callao, 123.

Calvert, Albert F., 39.

Camacho, Miguel Antonio, 132.

Campoamor:

   Absoluto, Lo, 7, 9, 20, 25, 30, 47, 59, 81, 84, 87, 89, 91-92, 94, 98, 106.

   Bacon, 6, 111.

   Cánovas, estudio biográfico, 22.

   Colón, 82, 100, 136, 138.

   Dies Irae, 59.

   Discurso en la Real Academia Española, 6, 17, 45, 89, 91-92, 99, 106, 141.

   Doloras, Las, 45, 90, 96, 117, 139.

   Drama universal, El, 118.

   Filisofía de las leyes, 5, 31, 34-35, 51, 53, 69, 91, 100, 123, 130, 140, 142.

   Guerra a la guerra, 7, 106, 141.

   Historia crítica de las cortes reformadoras, 5, 122, 137.

   Humoradas, 6.

   Ideísmo, El, 7, 22, 27, 29-30, 33, 37-38, 40, 46, 53, 66, 69, 82-83, 86, 89, 93, 111, 117-118, 136.

   Licenciado Torralba, El, 7, 115.

   Metafísica y la poesía, La, 25, 46, 111.

   Originalidad y el plagio, La, 119.

   Pequeños poemas, Los, 88, 117.

   Personalismo, El, 6, 9-14, 18, 20-22, 26, 28-36, 38, 40-41, 43-45, 48-50, 54-55, 57, 63-66, 68, 70, 72, 74, 77, 79-84, 87-89, 91-94, 97, 100-101, 103, 105-106, 108-110, 114-117, 119-121, 123, 130-131, 134, 138, 140.

   Poética, 31, 43, 46, 81, 110, 119, 122.

   Polémicas con la democracia, 11-12, 15 33, 39, 49, 54, 60, 64, 85, 95-96, 109, 112-113, 121-123, 138, 142.

   Polémicas sobre el panenteísmo, 75, 124.

Camusat de Riancey, C. L. de, 85.

Canalejas y Casas, Francisco de Paula, 10-11, 61, 123-127, 129.

Canova, 87.

Cánovas del Castillo, 21-23, 25, 124, 126-127.

Cantù, Cesare, 69.

Capuchins, 34.

Carducci, 34.

Carlism, 24, 36, 56, 58.

Carlos Quinto, 116-118.

Carlyle, 64.

Carmelites, 8.

Carmen, Cofradía del, 8.

Cartagena, 123.

Cartesianism. *See* Descartes.

Carthage, 35, 60.

Casas, las, 135.

Castelar, Emilio, 10-12, 18, 33, 39-40, 48-49, 60-62, 82, 95, 109, 112-113, 123, 142.

Castellón de la Plana, 6, 130.

Castile, 118, 136.

Catalonia, 96, 142.

Cato, 82.

Cejador y Frauca, Julio, 2, 5-6, 22.

Cervantes, 89, 110, 119.

Chamberlain, Houston Stewart, 69.

Charles V. *See* Carlos Quinto.

Chateaubriand, 32, 93-94.

Cherfils, Christian, 66.

Chile, 123.

China, 68, 71, 73, 75-76.

Choutard, J., 85.

Christ, 31-34, 79, 84, 91, 110, 136, 141.

Christina of Sweden, 90.

Cieszkowski, August, 66.

Cisneros, Jiménez de, 116.

"Clarín." *See* Alas, Leopoldo.

Clarke, H. Butler, 122-123.

Clemencín, Diego, 7.

Clement XIV, Pope, 40.

Clovis, 63.

Cochin-Chinese, 76.

Colorado, V., 1.

Columbus, 116, 138. *See also* Campoamor, *Colón*.

Comenge y Ferrer, Luis, 16.

Company of Jesus. *See* Jesuits.

Comte, Auguste, 22, 53.

Condorcet, 63, 66, 92-93.

Contemporáneo, El, 17-18, 25, 123.

Córdoba, 38.

Córdoba, Buenaventura de, 38.

Córdoba, Gonzalo de, 84, 136.

Corea. *See* Korea.

Coronado de Perry, Carolina, 45.

Cortes, las, 5, 36, 95, 122, 139.

Cortés, Hernán, 114, 136, 139.

Cossacks, 75.

Cresson, W. P., 75.

Croce, B., 67.
Crowest, Frederick J., 87.
Crusades, 79, 83.
Cuesta, Fernández, 61.
Cutanda, Vicente, 13.
Cuvier, 13-14, 69.

Dante, 31.
Dapper, Olfert, 72.
Darmon, Victor, 137.
Darwin, Charles, 14, 22-23.
Daubenton, 14.
Democracia, La, 39, 60, 62.
Desbassayns de Richemont, 85.
Descartes, 18, 21, 81, 89-90, 94, 99, 101, 124, 127.
Deutsche Annalen zur Kentniss der Gegenwart, 105.
Diana, 81, 104.
Dickstein, S., 66.
Diogenes, 40.
Discusión, La, 40, 60-62.
Drake, 112.
Dupanloup, F. A. P., 85.

Ebro, 96.
Egaña, Pedro, 131, 142.
Eichhorn, Johann A. F., 104.
Encyclopédie, 92, 111.
England, 68, 70-71, 77, 100, 108-113, 118, 135-137, 142.
Epoca, La, 123.
Erasmus, 115.
Escapulario, Cofradía del, 8.
Escorial, 39, 117, 120.
Escosura, Patricio de la, 85-86.
Eskimos, 74.
España, La, 142.
Espasa-Calpe, Enciclopedia, 2, 5-6, 22, 60.
Estado, El, 60, 62.

Felipe II, 39, 116-118.
Felipe IV, 118.
Ferdinand VII. *See* Fernando VII.
Fernández Bremón, José, 119.
Fernández Cuesta y Picatoste, Nemesio, 60-61.
Fernando VII, 3-4, 11.
Ferreres, Joaquín, 131.

Feuerbach, Ludwig, 51, 105.
Fichte, 26-27, 41, 102-104, 124.
Finns, 74.
Fisher, Sydney George, 57.
Flórez Estrada, Alvaro, 16.
Fouillée, Alfred, 21.
Fourier, 94.
France, 6, 12, 26, 43, 49, 61, 70-71, 77, 80, 83, 85, 88-99, 101, 112, 118, 120, 132, 137.
Francis I, 117.
Franklin, Benjamin, 57, 112.
Frederick the Great, 40.
Fuente, Vicente de la, 4, 30.

Gago, Francisco Mateos, 17.
Galicia, 3.
Galileo, 87.
Gallego, Juan Nicasio, 44.
Gándara y Navarro, José de la, 139.
García, Juan, 115.
García Icazbalceta, Joaquín, 135.
García de los Santos, Benito, 38.
Garibaldi, 96.
Gerbet, O. P., 85.
Germania, 105.
Germany, 6, 17, 20, 28-29, 50, 61, 70-71, 73-74, 80, 89, 92, 100-107, 108, 110, 113, 127, 134.
Ghengis Khan, 75.
Gibraltar, 137.
Giner de los Ríos, 24, 127-128.
Gioberti, 125.
Girardin, Emile de, 6.
Globo, El, 97-98.
Gobineau, 68-69, 72.
Goethe, 81, 103, 106.
Gómez Ocaña, José, 52.
Gómez Pereira, 89.
Goñi, Facundo, 123.
Gonnard, René, 59.
González Araco, Manuel, 10.
González Blanco, Andrés, 7, 35, 43, 68, 96-97, 99, 130, 133.
González Bravo, 133.
González Serrano, Urbano, 1, 24, 129.
González y Díaz Tuñón, Ceferino, 38, 40, 89.
Grandguillot, A. P., 85.

Great Britain. *See* England.
Greece, 60, 81-83.
Gregory XIII, Pope, 84.
Grevenbroek, Johannes Gulielmus de, 72.
Grondy, de, 85.
Grotius, 73.
Guad-el-Jelú, 79.
Guadalete, 78-79.
Guardiola, J. B., 142.
Guéronnière, de la, 85.
Guizot, 40.
Gumplovicz, 68, 138.

Hagenmeyer, H., 79.
Hannay, David, 10.
Hapsburgs, 83.
Hare, Christopher, 117.
Hegel, 32, 66, 103-105, 124.
Heine, 69.
Heraldo, El, 142.
Herbart, Johann F., 21, 48.
Herder, 66.
Herodotus, 87.
Herrera, Fernando de, 86, 119.
Herrera, Juan de, 39.
Herwegh, Georg, 105.
Hildreth, R., 76.
Hilton, Ronald, 1, 14, 22, 24.
Hindus, 77.
Hobroyd, Charles, 87.
Hochart, P., 82.
Hoene-Wronski, Josef Marja, 66.
Hohenemser, Richard, 53.
Hollander, J. H., 16.
Homer, 119.
Horace, 83.
Hottentots, 72.
Hoyos Sáinz, Luis de, 68.
Hugo, Victor, 12, 42, 51, 55, 97-98, 109, 136.
Hume, 110.
Huns, 75.
Hurtado y Valhondo, Antonio, 45.

Iberia, La, 40, 61-62.
Ilustración Española y Americana, 46.
Imparcial, El, 23.
India, 69, 71, 102.
Ingram, John Kells, 16.

Iroquois, 73.
Irula, 68.
Isabel II, 32, 58, 63, 121, 138.
Isabel la Católica, 84, 116, 118.
Isambert, Gaston, 50.
Islam, 78, 83.
Italy, 57, 71, 87, 96, 118.

Jackson, A. V. Williams, 15.
James, William, 28.
Japan, 73-74, 76.
Jérez, 137.
Jerusalem, 83.
Jesuits, 4, 12.
Jews, 71, 79, 84.
Job, 27.
John, King of England, 108.
Joly, Henry, 28.
Jouffory, 54.
Jovellanos, 4.
Joven España, La, 15.
Julius II, Pope, 84.
Jupiter, 81, 104.
Jussieu, 13.
Justinian, 104.

Kalmaks, 75.
Kalmak-Mongols, 71.
Kamchadeles, 74.
Kant, 21, 102, 106, 123, 125, 127.
Keane, A. H., 74.
Keuchel, G., 104.
Kirghiz, 75.
Kolarians, 68.
Korea, 74, 76.
Krause, 1, 8, 24, 75, 123-127, 129.
Kroeber, A. L., 68-69.

Laet, Johannes de, 73.
La Harpe, 40.
Lane-Poole, Stanley, 78.
Lange, 21.
Lapouge, 69.
Lapps, 74.
Larra, 120.
Lavoisier, Antoine, 13.
Lealtad, La, 24.
Leibnitz, 28.
Lema, Marqués de, 21.
Lemonnyer, J., 52.

Leo XII, Pope, 84.
Leo XIII, Pope, 31, 38.
Léon, Xavier, 27.
León, Luis de, 119.
León y Castillo, Fernando de, 35.
Leopardi, 41, 53.
Leroy-Beaulieu, Anatole, 75.
Linnæus, 13, 69.
Linterna, La, 24.
Lista, Alberto, 119.
Locke, 110.
London, 39.
Longford, Joseph H., 76.
Louis XIV, 63.
Louis-Philippe, 56, 95-96.
Lugan, A., 38.
Luther, Martin, 56-57, 59, 89, 101-102, 115, 134.
Lysimachus, 65.

Macaulay, Thomas Babington, 25, 111.
Macpherson, Hector, 14.
Madariaga, Salvador de, 48.
Madrazo, Federico de, 30.
Madrazo, Mariano de, 30.
Madrid, 4, 12, 29, 32, 43, 63, 132, 138.
Magyars, 74.
Mahomet, 40, 77.
Maistre, Joseph de, 111.
Malays, 71, 75.
Malebranche, 28, 91.
Malthus, 52.
Mani, 15.
Manrique, Jorge, 119.
Maria Cristina, Queen, 4, 87, 120-121.
Marmontel, 40.
Marr, Wilhelm, 105-106.
Martel y Fernández de Córdoba, Ricardo, 61.
Martínez de la Rosa, Francisco, 45, 137.
Martos Jiménez, Juan, 23, 60.
Martos y Balbí, Cristino, 6.
Mata y Fontanet, Pedro, 15.
Mateos, Nicomedes Martín, 94.
Mazade, Charles de, 6.
Mazzini, 106.
McKie, Douglas, 13.
Menéndez de Rayón, Damián, 10.
Menéndez y Pelayo, Marcelino, 9, 66-67, 89.

Mercedes, Queen of Spain, 122.
Merton, Reginald, 116.
Mexico, 68, 73, 135, 139.
Michael Angelo, 38, 86-87.
Michelet, 98.
Mignet, M., 117.
Miraflores, Cartuja de, 93.
Moi, 68.
Moleschott, Jacob, 22.
Molins, José Elías de, 38.
Molins, Marqués de, 45, 130, 137-138.
Moltke, 107.
Monaldeschi, 90.
Monforte, 64.
Mongols, 74-76.
Monlau, Pedro Felipe, 91.
Monóvar, 64.
Montesquieu, 5, 31, 34, 53, 56, 69, 91-92, 140.
Montijo, Eugenia María de, 96.
Montor, Artaud de, 84.
Montoro, Rafael, 128.
Morayta Sagrario, Miguel, 10.
Moreno, Domingo, 37.
Mormonism, 112.
Morocco, 136.
Morton, 69.
Moscow, 101.
Moses, 77, 86.
Murray, David, 76.

"Nakens," 97-98.
Napoleon I, 63, 88, 93-94, 96, 121, 136.
Napoleon III, 85, 88, 95-96, 112.
Narváez, 36.
Navarrete y Fernández Landa, Ramón, 45.
Navia, 3.
Nero, 82, 95.
Nettement, A. F., 85.
Newton, 110.
Nice, 86, 96.
Nielsen, Fredrik, 84.
Nikoltschoff, Wassil, 27.
Nisot, M. T., 52.
Nocedal, Cándido, 36-37, 133.
Norte, El, 128.
Novaya Zemlia, 74.
Novelda, 64.

Ochoa, Eugenio de, 97.
O'Donnell, Leopoldo, Duque de Tetuán, 61, 78, 86.
O'Donnell y Jorris, Enrique, 61.
O'Gorman, Guillermina, 7.
Okakura-Kakuzo, 76.
Omar, Caliph, 78.
Ordóñez, M., 1.
Origen, 40.
Orsini, M., 85.
Ortega y Gasset, 26, 142.
Ortiz de Pinedo, Abelardo, 23.
Ostyaks, 74.

Palacio, Manuel del, 60.
Palarea, José, 131.
Papacy, 56, 83, 85, 86, 120, 134.
Pardo-Bazán, 1, 39, 68, 79, 93, 100, 114, 138-139.
Paris, 35, 95, 97.
Parisis, P. L., 85.
Pascal, 87, 90-91.
Pellicer, 7.
Perry, Commodore, 76.
Persia, 82.
Peru, 123.
Philip. *See* Felipe.
Phoenicia, 60.
Pí y Margall, Francisco, 60, 62, 113.
Pidal, Pedro José, 44.
Pidal y Mon, Alejandro, 38, 45, 139.
Pilar de la Horadada, 29.
Pintado y Llorca, Ignacio, 24.
Pius IX, Pope, 84.
Pizarro, 136.
Plantier, C. H. A., 85.
Plato, 35, 40, 81, 119.
Pollen, J. H., 4.
Pons y Umbert, Adolfo, 21.
Portugal, 80, 136-137.
Pougin, A., 87.
Poujoulat, J. J. F., 85.
Prescott, William H., 84.
Prim, 78.
Pritchard, 69.
Propagador de la Libertad, El, 15.
Proudhon, Pierre-Joseph, 50.
Prussia, 100.
Puerto de Vega, 4.

Pygmalion, 81.
Pythagoras, 40.

Quatrefages, A. de., 69.
Quesnel, Léo, 2.
Quintana, 120.
Quixote, Don, 75, 119.
Raich, Maria, 26.
Rambla de Elda, 64.
Rattazzi, Mme., 10.
Razón, La, 142.
Redins, P., 85.
Regeneración, La, 24.
Renan, 21, 98.
Renouvier, Charles-Bernard, 9, 22.
Répide, Pedro de, 64.
Revilla y Moreno, Manuel de la, 7-8, 24, 120, 124, 126-129.
Revista Europea, 128.
Ricardo, David, 16.
Rickert, Heinrich, 27.
Ríos Rosas, 133.
Rivarol, 99.
Rivero, Nicolás María, 60, 62.
Robertson, J. M., 33.
Roca de Togores y Carrasco, Mariano. *See* Molins, Marqués de.
Rodríguez, Gabriel, 61, 72, 112.
Rodríguez Carracido, José, 23.
Rodríguez y Villalonga, 61.
Rome, 35, 55, 60, 78, 81-84, 109, 115, 134.
Roque Barcía, 9, 22.
Ros, 78.
Rosas, 138.
Rosebault, Charles J., 78.
Rosmini, 125.
Rossini, 87.
Roule, Louis, 13.
Roure y Figueras, Narciso, 38.
Rousseau, Jean Jacques, 29, 33, 50, 54, 92, 94.
Rubio y Collet, Carlos, 40, 61.
Rudolphi, 69.
Rumania, 80.
Russell, Bertrand, 28.
Russia, 100, 101.

Saint Bartholomew, Massacre of, 84.
Saint-Simon, 49, 94.

Saint-Vincent, Bory de, 69.
Saladin, 78.
Salamanca y Mayol, José de, Marqués de Salamanca, 64.
Saleilles, Raymond, 51.
Salmerón, Nicolás, 24, 127-128.
Samoyads, 74.
San Carlos, Real Colegio de Cirugía y Medicina de, 4.
San Luis, Conde de. *See* Sartorius, Luis José.
San Vicente, 64.
Sánchez, Miguel, 24.
Sánchez del Real, Andrés, 10.
Sand, George, 42.
Sandoval, F. de, 10.
Santiago de Compostela, 4, 30.
Santo Domingo, 139.
Santo Tomás, Academia de (*or* Colegio de), 4.
Santovenia, Emeterio S., 78.
Sanz del Río, 124-125.
Saragossa, 96.
Sartorius, Luis José, 11, 130, 142.
Savoy, 86, 96.
Savoy, House of, 86.
Say, Jean-Baptiste, 16.
Scandinavia, 71, 108.
Schelling, 103-104, 124.
Schiller, 106.
Schlegel, 66.
Schopenhauer, 53.
Sebastian, King of Portugal, 78.
Seillière, Ernest, 53.
Seligman, C. G., 72.
Senoi, 68.
Serban, N., 53.
Sevilla, 78.
Shakespeare, 110.
Siamese, 76.
Sidgwick, Henry, 33.
Sieiro González, Juan, 128.
Siglo Futuro, 24.
Smith, Adam, 16.
Socrates, 49, 133.
Solaro della Margherita, C., 85.
Soldevilla Ruiz, Fernando, 24.
Solsona, Conrado, 24.
Sorbonne, 19, 89.

Sparta, 109.
Spearman, 48.
Spencer, Herbert, 22, 110-111.
Spinoza, 20, 33, 41-43, 65, 79, 102, 104, 124, 127.
Stewart, Dugald, 51.
Stillman, W. J., 86.
Strauss, David Friedrich, 32, 105.
Sweden, 90, 108.
Symonds, John Addington, 86.

Tacitus, 82.
Talaings, 76.
Tamerlane, 75.
Tartars, 75.
Tartaro-Chinese, 76.
Taylor, I. A., 90.
Teatro Español, 11.
Teilhac, Ernest, 16.
Tello de Quirós, 59.
Ten Rhyne, Willem, 72.
Teresa de Jesús, Santa, 119.
Tetuán, 78-79.
Texcoco, 135.
Thales, 104.
Thomas Aquinas, Saint, 4, 20, 30, 37-38, 41.
Thucidides, 87.
Tibetans, 76.
Tiempo, El, 24, 128.
Toala, 68.
Tolosa, 96.
Tonnelli, Luigi, 53.
Topete, 122.
Torralba, Eugenio. *See* Campoamor, *Licenciado Torralba, El.*
Torrejón de Ardoz, 4.
Torres Cabrera, Conde de. *See* Martel y Fernández de Córdoba, Ricardo.
Troy, 81.
Trubetskoi, 85.
Tungus, 74.
Turanians, 75.
Turkey, 75, 140.

Ugarte de Ercilla, Eustaquio, 38.
Ulloa, Antonio de, 73.
Unamuno, 1, 14, 34, 50, 79, 81, 83, 92.
United States, 108-113, 121.

Valencia, 6, 32, 43, 132-133, 138.
Valencia, Duque de, 131.
Valera, Juan, 17-18, 25, 40, 45-46, 97-98.
"Vásquez," 97-98.
Vatican, 84.
Vedda, 68.
Vega, Lope de, 119.
Velásquez, 34.
Venegas, Miguel, 73.
Venice, 60, 140.
Venus, 81, 87, 104.
Verdi, 87.
Vico, 66-67.
Victor Emanuel, 86.
Vieira, Domingos, 44.
Villahermosa, Palacio de, 45.
Virey, 69.

Vizcaya, 96.
Voltaire, 28-32, 40, 42, 48, 50, 57-58, 63, 66, 78, 81, 91-92, 94, 111.

Waitz, 69.
Weinel and Widgery, 32.
Westermann, Dietrich, 72.
Wilhelm II, 74.
Wilson, Woodrow, 106.
Wordsworth, 60.

Yuste, 117.

Zahonero, José, 23.
Zaragoza, Señor, 43.
Zorrilla, 43.
Zumárraga, Juan de, 135.
Zurbitu, D., 39.

Milton Keynes UK
Ingram Content Group UK Ltd.
UKHW010334180724
445696UK00001B/52